Singleness, Marriage & being God's Family

Singleness, Marriage & Being God's Family
© Ian Blight 2023

ISBN 978-0-6459169-0-4

Cover image: Pixabay | Antonio López Velasco
Cover design and interior diagrams: Ben Morton for Immortalise
Editor: Valerie Williams
Interior typeset and design: Beckon Creative

 A catalogue record for this book is available from the National Library of Australia

For all scripture quotations, unless otherwise indicated:
All scripture quotations, unless otherwise indicated, are taken from the Holy Bible, New International Version®, NIV®. Copyright© 1973, 1978, 1984 and 2011 Biblica, Inc.®. Used by permission of Zondervan. All rights reserved worldwide www.zondervan.com. The "NIV" and "New International Version" are trademarks in the United States Patent and Trademark Office by Biblica, Inc.®

For scripture quotations followed by 'ESV':
Scripture quotations are from the ESV Bible (The Holy Bible, English Standard Version®), Copyright© 2001 Crossway, a publishing ministry of Good News Publishers. Used by permission. All rights reserved.

For scripture quotations followed by 'NKJV':
Scripture quotations are from the New King James Version®. Copyright© 1982 Thomas Nelson. Used by permission. All rights reserved.

For scripture quotations followed by 'KJV2000':
Scripture quotations are taken from the King James Version 2000. Copyright© 2000 Dr Robert A. Couric. Published by the Bible League. Used by permission. All rights reserved.

Singleness, Marriage & being God's Family

Ian Blight

Acknowledgements

Many people, through their time and efforts, have kindly and generously supported the production of this book. I acknowledge my reliance on their contributions and assistance, and appreciate the support received, whether throughout this writing project or at critical times when it was needed.

I am grateful to Valerie Williams for her editing and for giving direction and guidance in a very patient and encouraging way. As this has been my first major writing project, I have needed much guidance and assistance, especially at the beginning. I cannot thank Valerie enough for the help she has given.

Special thanks go to Fleur Hourihan, Nicole Hancock, the National Church Life Survey (NCLS) Research team and the NCLS Research sub-committee for the facilitation and compilation of the NCLS Report and for the ongoing research that has enabled this report to be produced. This report, included as an appendix, contributed to the initial impetus for writing this book and has provided substance for discussion.

Rev Bryce Clark generously gave assistance and advice on the improving of my early draft manuscript. I would like to convey my sincere thanks to him for the direction he provided.

I am much indebted to Rev Frank Tucker for his assistance in reviewing my draft manuscript. His experience and knowledge have been invaluable and I am grateful for his guidance and advice.

I would like to express my appreciation to Ben Morton for his patience and advice in working toward creating the cover design and publishing this book. Thanks also to Dot Turner for generously assisting with much of the background work which began the process of choosing the cover design and title.

I would like to thank Rebekah Robinson of Beckon Creative for her thoroughness and timeliness in the typesetting of this book for publication.

Many others have generously given their time and assistance in varying aspects of producing this book. Comments and feedback from some people helped me to improve the draft manuscript and book cover design. Others have introduced me to reference books and articles that have been important sources of information. A valuable contribution has been the creation and modifying of figures and graphs for inclusion in the book.

I acknowledge, and am grateful for, the various copyright permissions given so I could use the work of others in producing this book.

This book could not have been completed without the assistance and support that has kindly been given. I greatly appreciate the support and wholeheartedly say *thank you* to all of these people.

Foundations

Contents

Introduction	**15**
Families and singles in the church	16
A conversation	18
The big picture in Australia	22
***Chapter 1: A Review of* Being Single**	**25**
Historical–sociological overview	26
Pre-Christian Celts	26
Christian influence	27
The Reformation — Europe	29
The British Isles — Puritans	30
The British Isles — 'Christian humanism'	32
Influence of capitalism	33
The Victorian novel	34
Declining influence of the church	35
1960 to the present	36
The church's response to social change	37
Consequences for single people	37
A biblical perspective of singleness	38
Modelling a way forward	40
Review summary	41

Chapter 2: Secular Wisdom and God's Wisdom — 43
- Social change — 44
  - Underlying issues — 45
- God's higher wisdom — 46
  - The omission of the cross — 48
  - An illustration of what God says — 49
- Effect of marriage on well-being — 51
- Contrast of the secular approach — 54
  - Social philosophies — 55
  - Spectrum of secular ideas — 56
  - Problems at both ends — 59
  - Starting at the centre — 61
- The church — precious to God — 63
- Enemies of God and His people — 64
- The well-being of the church — 65
- Building on the rock — 65

Chapter 3: Foundations — 67
- Defining love — 67
- Factors influencing change — 68
- Two distinct approaches — 69
  - A biblical approach — 70
  - A secular approach — 71
- Detrimental to the church — 72
- Marriage and families replacing Christ — 73
  - Building blocks of society — 74
  - Foundational institution of society — 75
  - Foundation of society — 77
  - A flourishing society — 83
  - Holding nations together — 83
  - The greatest hope of humanity — 84

Flow-on effect	84
Love within families	86
The converse situation	87
Detrimental to marriage and families	88

Chapter 4: A Broader View — 91

Elements of marriage	92
The natural family	94
The family and persecution	95
As goes the family, so goes the nation	96
Members of our household	98
Link between self and family	99
The measure of faith	100
Looking to the future	101
What is normal?	102

Chapter 5: The Image of God — 103

A significant concept	104
The image of God	105
Attributes	106
Implications	107
Relevance today	108
Classifying the interpretations	109
A relational view	109
A functional view	110
A substantive view	113
Interpretations of Genesis 1:27	113
Included in the image of God	114
Not included in the image of God	115
The image of the invisible God	116
Diverse interpretations	117
What the image of God does not mean	118

Chapter 6: An Overview of God's Plan — 121
- Overview — the Fall — 122
- God's promises to Abraham — 124
- Moses and the Passover — 128
- God's promise to David — 129
- Prophecy — 130
- Foretelling fulfilled — 132
- The outcome of God's plan — 134
- The first Adam and the last Adam — 134
- Hope of Israel — 135
- Reflection — 136

Chapter 7: The Beginning and the 'Last Days' — 139
- Natural then spiritual — 140
- The last days — 140
- A new birth — 141
- A different perspective on family — 143
- No longer alone — 144
  - Helper — 145
  - Alone does not mean single — 147
- Fruitfulness — 148
  - No exemption — 148
- The family of God is one body — 151
- A greater blessing — 152
- Slavery and freedom — 154

Chapter 8: Dealing with the Cause — 157
- Trusting that God is good — 158
- Ministry of reconciliation — 160

Delight in God's law	160
Categories of biblical law	162
Revealing sin	163
Our inability to fully observe God's law	163
Following God's law	164
A social trend	165
Progression	166
A pressing concern	166
Prior to the change	167
The change and the response	169
Initiation of the problem	170
Impact on singleness	171
Shield of faith	172
The contemporary situation	173
Self-perpetuating cycle	174
Chapter 9: Being Single in God's Family	**177**
Is being single a gift?	178
When God gives	181
Not a spiritual gift	182
Evaluating the interpretations	184
The world's misleading wisdom	188
Looking further	191
God chooses us	192
The wedding banquet	193
God chooses the lowly	196
People of faith	197
Seeing things differently	198
The psalmist's experience	199
Tough love	203

Chapter 10: Closing Reflections   207
   The dilemma   207
   Oblivious   208
   Ambient acceptance   210
   New challenges   211
   Looking forward   213
   God's guidance   215
   Final word   216

Appendix   219
   Australian singles — A church and community comparison (NCLS Research)   220

Notes   235

Bibliography   249

Index   255

LIST OF FIGURES

Chapter 2

Figure 2.1: The spectrum of secular ideas on the value of marriage and families within society   57

Figure 2.2: Dealing with sin through faith in Christ, and trusting in God's word, adds a different dimension to finding a solution to the social problems we are facing   61

Chapter 4

Figure 4.1: Marriages performed in Australia by ministers of religion compared to those performed by civil celebrants   93

Introduction

'Someone should write something about this' was a nagging thought that would recur from time to time. One of those occasions was after I had been communicating for a while with a young woman interstate, with whom I had become acquainted through a friend in Sydney. She had written to me about her deep feelings of abandonment within the church. She had previously been married and experienced great love and support in her church fellowship. The stark contrast of how she, as a single person in her thirties, was now received, had left her feeling isolated and disillusioned. This heartfelt expression of her feelings and emotions resonated within me, not because I had previously experienced life within a church fellowship as a married person, but because I had observed and experienced how single people were often treated differently. Naturally, married people and single people often have different interests and socialise in different ways, but the real issue was something deeper.

Having worked and lived in numerous regions across two states for several years, I had enjoyed the fellowship of various churches of different denominations as I was transferred from place to place. Always in a church, some would be very supportive of single people, but often something rooted deep within the church culture and mindset made a single person feel they did not fit in. I was beginning to experience this feeling more and more as time went on.

I have since returned on a more permanent basis to my home state of South Australia. Here, over a period of several years, I experienced a few instances of what seemed to be over-exuberant support for the position of marriage and families within the church. The unintended consequence was to devalue the position of single people. Jesus, however, inspires honour for both singleness and marriage (Romans 12:10). To Him, single people are loved and valued no less than any other.

Families and singles in the church

The topic of marriage and families and their position in society has been well discussed for many years. Convincing and fine-sounding human thinking can be found offering solutions to the problems experienced. Numerous ideas and philosophies can be found which aim to bring peace and stability wherever damage and instability have occurred.

In evaluating these ideas and philosophies, their impact on those who are single should be considered. However, this is not always done. The way in which the position of marriage and families is viewed greatly impacts on single people and their position within the church and society.

In contrast to our own reasoning, God tells us of His thoughts, saying, 'As the heavens are higher than the earth, so are my ways higher than your ways and my thoughts than your thoughts' (Isaiah 55:9). This is as true for the topic of marriage, family and singleness as it is for any other matter. Many of the ideas circulating in society advocate for marriages and families to be given preferential and favoured treatment, supposedly for the benefit of society as a whole. These ideas, however, come from our own human reasoning. Wherever marriage and families are given an elevated position, whether within the church or in wider society, in my experience, this leads to unintended detrimental consequences for single people. In contrast to these ideas, God's righteous ways lead to equal concern for each other, whether married or single (1 Corinthians 12:25).

It is reasonable to think that a single person could contribute to the discussion on the topic of marriage, family and singleness in a way that those who are married could not. Within the church, we have the benefit of the wisdom of God's word in dealing with the situations we face. However, in the area of marriage and family, there is a contrary influence to contend with: the weight of secular reasoning. The broader perspective offered by a single person can only be beneficial in navigating the discussion as a whole, especially within the church.

A conversation

Some works of literature, to which I refer in this book, specifically identify singleness within the church as an issue needing attention. Or, at least, they highlight the need for an ongoing conversation on marriage, family and singleness.

Philip B. Wilson (2005), in his book *Being Single — Insights for Tomorrow's Church,* investigates the experience of single people in the church within the British Isles. In his evaluation, Wilson indicates the further need for discussion about the issue of singleness within society and the church. He finds that, in general, the church has not been a good place for single people. However, he suggests that the church is still the best forum in which to discuss the issues faced in life as a single person, and that the church could be one of the best places for a single person to be.[1]

In Millard J. Erickson's (2013) book, *Christian Theology,* the author includes discussion on the topic of people who are unmarried in American society. The tendency of American society to pay higher regard to the state of marriage over that of singleness is reflected in the church. He observes that, consequently, the unmarried person often does not fit into the life and culture of American churches.²

Andreas J. Köstenberger and David W. Jones (2010) discuss marriage and families in their book, *God, Marriage and Family: Rebuilding the Biblical Foundation*. My impression is that they provide their view of biblical theology from a pro-family perspective. Although their work is also based in the United States, their comments about single people are more generalised. They state that post-adolescent singles are probably the most overlooked and marginalised social group in the Western church.³

Australian author, Kevin Andrews (2012), in his book, *Maybe I Do: Modern Marriage & the Pursuit of Happiness*, in my view, also presents a pro-family perspective. He has examined an extensive range of global social research from the 1960s and following decades, and commented on the results. Andrews also appears to envisage the need for further discussion on the topic of marriage and the family in society, including the issue of singleness. In his book's introduction, he states that the purpose of his writing is to examine and draw from social science research in a way that could inform further discussion.⁴

National Church Life Survey (NCLS) researcher, Fleur Hourihan (2023), in her research paper, 'Australian Singles — A Church and Community Comparison,' examines statistical data relating to singleness and the Australian church. She observes that an increasing number of Australian adults find themselves outside of marriage, with this same demographic under-represented in the church in Australia. She suggests this important matter should prompt discussions within the church.[5]

Since the 1960s and 1970s, governments and churches in Australia have sought to deal with problems emanating from the social change which has been experienced. Most of the conversation and cases being presented are from a marriage and family perspective. The conclusions arrived at by secular researchers, as presented by Andrews, are family focused. This presents a good opportunity to develop a conversation about singleness by presenting the 'other side' of the issues, that is, from the perspective of someone who is single.

Andrews provides a limited biblical perspective on some issues; however, most of the research and resulting conclusions are from the perspective of professional social researchers without any specific biblical or Christian insights. Through Andrews' work and the background supplied by Wilson, the opportunity to develop a conversation on these issues arises in which biblical wisdom is contrasted with the secular approach.

The social and moral causes and impacts of the social change are complex in nature. It is important to examine them from differing angles and perspectives when searching for solutions. In examining the issues from both a biblical perspective and that of a single person, my interpretations of, and conclusions on, the social research differ, at times, from those presented by Andrews. However, within both the church and society, engaging in the discussion from various angles is important for weighing up ideas and determining the most appropriate approach to address the issues involved. I acknowledge the valuable work of Andrews in his examination of the social research and its findings, which has facilitated the conduct of a more complete discussion than would otherwise have occurred.

This book's discussion frequently mentions families. It is acknowledged that everyone has a family of origin. Everyone has parents and maybe siblings. However, not everyone has a spouse and children. Wherever families are mentioned in discussion, the reference is to parents with children. Issues discussed in relation to singleness are naturally relevant to those who have never married. Many of the issues relating to singleness will also apply to those who have experienced broken marriages or who have been widowed, and may be relevant to those who are separated, although officially married, and to childless couples.

The big picture in Australia

To be aware of instances in which single people are marginalised within the church is sufficient to initiate concern. However, this awareness leads to another question. Is this a widespread occurrence and, if so, to what extent? In Australia, a valuable resource to turn to for further investigation of this question is the *National Church Life Survey*. This resource greatly assists efforts to quantify what is happening on a broad scale across the country. The NCLS is a census of the church population undertaken every five years, coinciding with the years in which the Australian Bureau of Statistics (ABS) conducts Australia's national census.

With much-appreciated backing from the Research Sub-committee, NCLS researcher Fleur Hourihan kindly agreed to compile a report titled 'Australian Singles — A Church and Community Comparison' (2023). She investigated the situation of single people in the church in Australia using the NCLS, with the ABS census of population and housing and the ABS national census as background and for comparison. Her report is referred to throughout this book and is included as an appendix.

A random statistical snapshot of church life once every five years has some limitations in revealing what is happening within the church. However, when a matter of significant concern is indicated in this snapshot, it does provide reasons for asking further questions. The NCLS report shows that single people are under-represented within the church community compared to their corresponding demographic in the wider Australian society. Conversely, married people are over-represented. From another angle, it could be said that married and single people are both greatly under-represented in the church today as a proportion of the national population, compared to the data from fifty or more years ago.[6] Although the report identifies that single people are under-represented within the church, it is evident that many single people are still found in the church.

The 1960s and 1970s brought a wave of cultural change, with its momentum continuing to the present time. Trends within the Australian population that illustrate this change include a decline of affiliation with the Christian religion and an increase in identifying with 'no religion.'[7] Other trends include an increased proportion of the population remaining single and an increased rate of separation and divorce.[8] In dealing with the social change, for the church to simply adjust to the prevailing mindset and culture within the secular community is not the way forward. A more appropriate way to approach these issues would be to follow the apostle Paul's advice. In valuing sound doctrine, Paul advised Timothy to act with 'great patience and careful instruction' (2 Timothy 4:2). This equally applies to the church today.

The intention of this book's discussion is not to provide definitive answers to the problems presented, but to work toward finding answers. God's ways are higher than our ways and we do not always perceive, at first, exactly what God is saying. This discussion presents a perception of what God is saying in His word about these issues, from a plain reading of scripture and from the perspective of a single person, to help work toward finding the truth on these issues.

Chapter 1

A Review of Being Single

The book, *Being Single — Insights for Tomorrow's Church*, by Philip B. Wilson (2005), provides a background to, and builds an understanding of, the current cultural climate as it affects single people in the church today. The book emanated from research carried out as part of the author's PhD studies at Aberdeen University while studying for ordination in the Presbyterian Church of Ireland. In his book, Wilson explores the historical, sociological and theological aspects of being single in the Christian church in the British Isles. In examining the current situation, he observes that many single people find that the church is not a good place for them to be.[1] Even though his investigation is based in the British Isles, its findings apply more widely to other Western countries. Despite single people often being marginalised within the church, Wilson argues that the church still offers the best forum for discussion of the issues faced by those who are single.[2]

The background and insights presented by Wilson provide a good basis on which to continue the conversation relating to singleness within the church. To facilitate further discussion, this chapter summarises and reviews some of the main points made by Wilson.[3]

Historical-sociological overview

Wilson first investigates the historical changes in the ways that single people have been treated by society and the church.[4] The Celts in pre-Christian Ireland are the starting point for his historical reflections.

Pre-Christian Celts

Living alone as a single person was an unknown situation in the pre-Christian Celtic community. People at that time did not live in a 'nuclear family' that we know today. With their family groups based on males with a common great-grandfather, everyone lived as part of an extended family group, with celibacy almost unknown. The morality of their community is described by Wilson as meandering and fluid.[5] No child was considered illegitimate, as almost all probabilities were considered acceptable.

Christian influence

The arrival of Christianity brought new ideas of morality and sexual ethics, including that of celibacy. Although Christianity remained a minority religion for some time, the rise of the Irish monastery as an institution was significant in influencing how singleness was viewed within the church and wider society. By the beginning of the sixth century, monasticism was central to the practice of Christianity throughout the British Isles.[6]

For an individual who chose a life of chastity within a monastery, initially it was not uncommon to attract family pressure and ridicule. Reasons included the individual being viewed as failing to carry out the purpose for which God created both genders, and the failure to provide the family with grandchildren.[7] However, monasteries offered a valid option for a single life. They provided the opportunity for advancement as a single person and ensured their members' financial security. They offered a good pathway to education, a supportive community and a means for the pursuit of eternal life.[8] Monasteries became very wealthy. For many single people, few advancement opportunities were available outside the monastery.

Wilson reflects on how monasteries influenced attitudes toward single people in later generations and later centuries.[9] He also draws on the model of relationships developed within monasteries that could be useful today for single people seeking authentic expressions of Christian living. He comments on the importance placed on a type of relationship referred to as a 'soul friendship' from about the ninth century. This friendship involved an older monk befriending a younger monk to develop a spiritually supportive 'father-like' relationship.

Under the Christian influence, marriage began to develop into a form resembling what is recognisable today. Priests and bishops began to become more involved in officiating at weddings. The importance and significance of marriage within the church advanced to the point where, by the thirteenth century, it was commonly regarded as a sacrament. Marriage symbolises the union between Christ and the church, this being the basis for it to become a sacrament. As a sacrament, marriage was viewed as a means of salvation for men and women in the medieval church.[10]

The monastery movement developed in a manner that protected the power and privilege of the institutional church. The church venerated singleness and celibacy within monasticism on one hand and the sacrament of marriage on the other. Unmarried people in the church, but members of neither a monastery nor a convent, were viewed with doubt and suspicion from both sides. Wilson comments that these single people would undoubtedly have had both their spirituality and 'normality' questioned. He suggests their situation may be somewhat recognisable by those who observe how singleness within the church is viewed today.[11]

The Reformation — Europe

Wilson next reflects on the Reformation in Europe, and its influence on the development of cultural attitudes toward marriage, the family and singleness.[12] Martin Luther, who became an Augustinian monk at twenty-two years of age, was a key figure of the Reformation. Luther's idea of the need for faith to attain salvation eventually led to a change in how practices within the church of that time were viewed. Practices, such as selling indulgences and revering the church and its hierarchy, were no longer considered adequate for finding peace with God. In response to this, Reformed churches reviewed the sacraments, with only baptism and communion remaining as sacraments. Five other sacraments, including marriage, were dismissed. However, the Roman Catholic tradition continued to recognise seven sacraments.

Wilson also suggests that Luther contributed significantly to altering how the family unit was perceived within society.[13] Luther left the monastery and married a former nun at a time when monasteries had become associated with all that was most displeasing within the medieval church. The institutional church's power base, centred in monasteries, was curtailed in the Reformation. While monasticism continued, expressions of piety and worship previously expected within the domain of a monastery, were brought by Luther into normal family life, a model which influenced many people. Luther's model has often been linked to the development of the form of family life known as 'the nuclear industrial' family.

Although the church historically found certainty in its position on salvation and Christian living, Wilson suggests that no such certainty was found in its position on marriage and singleness.[14] The Protestant church of the Reformation possibly overreacted to the Roman Catholic Church's teaching of clerical celibacy. It sought to resolve the ambiguity by regarding married life as the norm for everyone. Wilson suggests that, in hindsight, this may have been a mistake.[15] Resolving the matter in this way was possibly suitable at the time, but would later prove problematic for the church as singleness increased in future times.

The British Isles — Puritans

Wilson next turns to factors influencing cultural attitudes from within the British Isles at about the time of, and following, the Reformation.[16] He identifies the Puritan, John Bunyan (1628—1688), as one who significantly influenced attitudes toward marriage and singleness. The views held by Bunyan on these aspects of life were not greatly dissimilar to those of Luther.

Pilgrim's Progress, the famous allegory written by Bunyan in 1678, was a unique work of literature at that time and influenced many later literary works. The allegory describes the road to personal salvation for Christian, the leading character. It also incorporates a type of family salvation when Christian's wife and four children join him in the Celestial City.

The Puritans, as a religious community, placed great importance on family life and on marriage taking precedence over singleness. This is reflected in the allegory of *Pilgrim's Progress*. Wilson highlights one of Bunyan's characters, Gaius, who instructs Christian's wife, Christiana, regarding the importance of marriage for her sons. Gaius gives the reason that 'the Name of their Father, and the House of his Progenitors may never be forgotten in the World.'[17] The Puritans viewed marriage as a vocation. They considered it necessary for a man to be called by God to choose a wife in the same way that a person would be called by God to a particular profession.[18]

One of the key developments, identified by Wilson, regarding Christian living within the British Protestant Church in the seventeenth and eighteenth centuries, was 'the sanctification of the family into the people of God.'[19] The identification and development of the household as an individual spiritual unit was due, in part, to the Puritans. Thus, households became viewed as important to spiritual practice in ways that had previously been the case only for monasteries.

The British Isles — 'Christian humanism'

Although the Puritans influenced how society viewed the function of a family, Wilson suggests they may not have been the originators of many of the influential ideas.[20]

Widely throughout Europe in the seventeenth and eighteenth centuries, the form of the family was developing in similar ways to that within the British Protestant Church. This occurred even in places not influenced by the Puritans and the Reformation. Wilson refers to the views of commentator Margo Todd.[21] She suggests that the changes in how the family was perceived in the British Protestant Church matched the direction taken in the sixteenth century by Catholic humanist thought on the family. This clearly supports the theory that influences, other than those of the Reformation and the Puritans, were at work in transforming the European-wide cultural view of the family. These changes led to a form of the family now known as the 'nuclear family.'

Margo Todd (1987), writing in *Christian Humanism and the Puritan Social Order,* detects the significant influence of Christian humanist thought in the writings and practices of the Puritans. Dutch philosopher, Erasmus, was particularly influential on their thinking. The views of the Christian humanists, in turn, were influenced by other philosophical thought, including that of Aristotle.[22]

Aristotle viewed the family as the 'basic building block' of the whole of society; thus, the family was necessary for *eudaimonia*.[23] The Greek word, *eudaimonia*, describes 'human flourishing,' 'well-being,' 'a good life,' or 'being happy, healthy and prosperous.' Based on this observation, Wilson comments on how, without much difficulty, a correlation could be seen between Aristotle and the view that many Protestant churches held, and continue to hold, about the benefits of marriage.[24]

Influence of capitalism

The development of the 'nuclear family' was further advanced by the rising influence of capitalism. Factories, free markets, women's new role in the labour force, advances in technologies and agricultural mechanisation together precipitated a revolution in how families were organised, according to Wilson.[25] Instead of community-based agriculture, where those within a community helped each other with seasonal tasks, families developed into households more contained in nature and self-sufficient.

In these households, the major role of the mother was in the home with the children, while the father had the role of earning the family's income. Grown children who remained unmarried tended to remain in the family home, with few other options available and little consideration generally given to the concept of living alone.[26]

The Victorian novel

During the Victorian era, the 63-year period from 1837—1901 that marked the reign of England's Queen Victoria, authors like the Bronte sisters and Charles Dickens inspired the popularity of the novel. The novel became influential in determining what was defined as 'normality' by the community.[27] The image of normality thus created was invariably connected in some way to a love affair, with marriage being the desired destination and purpose in life.[28] During this era, marriage was perceived less in terms of the Puritan view of a vocation, but more, as identified by Wilson, in terms of its 'romanticism, respectability and advancement.'[29]

One concept drawn from Bunyan's *Pilgrim's Progress* was the desire to progress and advance: thus, for a single person, entering married life was viewed as progress. This concept had a significant influence on the world view portrayed in many Victorian novels.[30] Early Hollywood films followed the same sentiment. In an increasingly secular world, it was not Popes or preachers, but the novel that was the major force in shaping people's views about singleness and marriage.[31] Bunyan, in *Pilgrim's Progress*, modelled a particular way of viewing a successful life, with change, advancement, development and improvement all regarded as essential elements.[32]

A Review of Being Single

For single people, especially women, service in the field of Christian overseas missions could provide a sense of purpose and worth not readily available at home.[33] From 1800 onwards, single missionaries achieved great things and were highly regarded within the church. For Victorian Protestant single women, Wilson equates serving in overseas Christian missions with the position of the monastery for the Irish Celts.[34]

Declining influence of the church

In the nineteenth century, most of the British Isles' population had some association with the Christian church. However, as Wilson highlights, although Christianity was popular and important for most people, its prominence in their lives was beginning to decline.[35] Contentious matters arose which were challenging to the Christian faith, such as the 1859 publication of Charles Darwin's *On the Origin of Species by Means of Natural Selection*.

Across the British Isles, entertainment venues were growing in number. Mass-produced goods were becoming increasingly available. This period, at around 1800, was described as the 'first consumer society'.[36] As a cohesive influence for the whole of society, the church was beginning to decline. Wilson observes that the decline of marriage also began in the nineteenth century.[37] He traces the evidence and influencing factors of these trends.

1960 to the present

With radical changes in social thinking in the 1960s, the numerical decline of the church escalated. The increasing influence of post-modernist thought in the 1960s exerted pressure on institutionalism which significantly affected the institutions of marriage and the church. Marriage became less popular and those who married had less successful marriages. Singleness, as a preferred lifestyle option, became increasingly popular.[38]

Wilson identifies factors that influenced the broad changes in social thinking from the 1960s. They include a shift away from an industrial based economy; greater reliance on the services sector; a technological shift toward computer processes and away from mechanical processes; an increase in communications technology (TVs, computers, mobile phones, etc.); greater interest in relational spirituality; and decline in respect for organised religious institutions.[39] Other factors that affected relations between genders included the ready availability of contraception; the advent of no-fault divorce; and moves toward equal pay and employment opportunities for women. In ways previously unknown in human history, women were now becoming less reliant on men for their survival, and marriage was becoming more a lifestyle option than a necessity.[40]

The church's response to social change

Wilson suggests that numerical declines, particularly since the 1960s, in both marriage and church membership appear to have been caused by similar pressures and changes in the world view within society. He adds that most British churches responded by giving greater attention to promoting and supporting the traditional nuclear family unit. Wilson also provides examples of the same response by the church in the US and by the Roman Catholic Church.[41]

While families are commonly supported and promoted in British churches, Wilson finds that support is not extended, to the same degree, to single people. Although some initiatives support single people within the church, Wilson concludes that the church is not a welcoming or comforting place for many single Christian people.[42]

Consequences for single people

Wilson next reports on personal interviews he conducted that related to singleness and the church.[43] Fifteen people were interviewed, with those involved forming a wide cross-section of the church community. In analysing the interviews, although exceptions were found, Wilson identifies that many experienced difficulties in being single within the church.[44] 'Church-stress' and 'church-pain' are terms he uses to describe their experience.[45] In the responses received, some stated that it was easier to be single in wider society than in the church.[46]

Delving into people's experiences in his interviews, Wilson also observes that many single people have become isolated within church communities.[47] He highlights the point that most Protestant church leaders are married. Consequently, they appear to be ignorant of the issues faced by single people.[48] He suggests that the church could potentially be a place of significant value for single people; however, at present, churches seem to add to the problems of single people rather than resolving them.[49] He concludes that, for God's mission to be fulfilled, the church must gain an understanding of what to believe about singleness and of appropriate participation by single people in the life of the church.[50]

A biblical perspective of singleness

Wilson continues by investigating the biblical basis for reaching an understanding of singleness.[51] Three eras in the biblical record that are of significance for singleness are explored by Wilson. Each era provides a different perspective; however, when considered together, they assist with an understanding of what is important today.

The first era, described within the Hebrew scriptures, is largely based on God's promise to Abraham to give him many descendants.[52] For the Israelites, having children was a sign of success and of being blessed by Yahweh, while being childless represented failure. To live on through one's children was an individual's greatest hope in death. Consequently, single people had no real place within the Old Testament biblical culture.[53]

The second era is the time when Jesus lived among us.[54] Rather than God's people being physical descendants of Abraham, the apostle Paul speaks of Abraham as '… the father of us all' (Rom 4:16). Abraham's children are now children by faith rather than by blood. Jesus says, 'my mother and my brothers are those who hear God's word and put it into practice' (Luke 8:21). His resurrection gives those with faith in Him a hope beyond death, a hope shared by both the childless and those with children.[55] Jesus does not distinguish between married and single people. Both are among His associates. He clearly teaches that following Him is of far greater importance than family bonds (Luke 14:26; Matthew 10:37).

The third era relates to the remainder of the New Testament. In 1 Corinthians 7, Paul teaches that, as time is short, it is good if a person does not marry so they can be devoted to the Lord's work. Wilson suggests that it would not be common for contemporary Christians to think of the imminence of Christ's return as a reason why they ought not to marry.[56] Wilson argues that Paul twice says that he is stating his own opinion, not the Lord's, when writing on this topic. Instead of using what Paul says to centre the theology about singleness in the church, Wilson suggests that we should be centred on Jesus' life and teaching to guide our thinking.[57] During this third era, finds Wilson, singleness in the church is affirmed, with marriage not regarded as an essential part of Christian life.

Modelling a way forward

Finally, Wilson proposes some elements of a supportive church community that could be used to include all people, irrespective of their marital status or natural family ties.[58] Wilson suggests that the church should embrace singleness as a valid lifestyle, as it does with marriage and family life. Wilson highlights, however, that each church is different, with varying influences, inspirations and preferences. Thus, he does not consider it appropriate to prescribe a model for how a church could value and care for all people, including single people. It is not a case of 'one size fits all'.[59]

Wilson quotes contemporary American Christian ethicist, Stanley Hauerwas. Wilson agrees with the opinion stated by Hauerwas that one of the most important political concerns facing the Christian church in the twenty-first century is that of discerning the positions of singleness and the family.[60]

Review Summary

In his book *Being Single — Insights for Tomorrow's Church*, Wilson (2005) investigates the history of society in the British Isles. He traces the roots of the beliefs and attitudes which shape the way that marriage, the family and singleness are viewed today in society and the church. By building an understanding of how the present situation has arisen, he provides a platform from which to better address the issues and construct a vision for the future. The benefits of his insights and findings have a wider application than solely to the British Isles. The broader Western church in particular, would find value in them.

Wilson's discussions are not merely theoretical. He brings a very practical reality by conducting personal interviews which contribute insights and experience from a range of church members. His interviews reveal experiences and feelings that are cause for concern. He describes listening to those experiences as 'extremely discouraging'.[61] He concludes that, for many single people, the church is not a good place to be. Wilson's discussion is grounded in reality by delving into people's freely shared experiences, thus equipping and enabling us to discuss and deal with this topic from an informed position.

Importantly, Wilson also undertakes a substantial exploration of the biblical treatment of singleness. Ultimately, this provides the only sound framework for approaching the topic of singleness and for discussing the position of single people within the church.

Wilson builds an understanding of where the church is today and how it came to be where it is with respect to the place of singleness. He then develops a framework for moving forward. He discusses practical suggestions for how a church could better function as a caring and supportive community for everyone involved, including single people. Although Wilson proposes useful suggestions in the concluding section of his book, the reader is left with a sense that the conversation about singleness within the church remains open. Wilson concludes that one of the most pressing issues for the Christian church in the twenty-first century is how it deals with singleness and the family.[62] He argues that the church offers the best forum in which to discuss the issues for those who are single.[63] In saying this, Wilson appears to indicate the need for a wider and ongoing conversation on this subject. The strength of Wilson's book is that it establishes a platform and framework for this further discussion, both within local churches and at a wider church and societal level.

Chapter 2

Secular Wisdom and God's Wisdom

Fleur Hourihan's (2023) NCLS report, *Australian Singles — A Church and Community Comparison* [the 'NCLS Report'] examines the number of people attending churches in Australia in each of the years in which the survey was conducted. It reveals the proportions of people differentiated by their marital status within the Australian church community. Comparing these results with the national census data, the NCLS Report shows that single people are under-represented within the Australian church compared to their corresponding demographic within wider Australian society.[1] Even taking de facto marriage relationships into account, single people are still significantly under-represented within the church. This is particularly evident in the middle years from approximately thirty-five to sixty-five years of age.[2] Even though not all single people are alienated from the church, these statistics suggest that many are. An important question to ask is: why is this occurring and how can it be remedied?

Wilson has investigated the experience of single people in the church in the British Isles. He describes how some people in the church view marriage and family as an essential part of the Christian faith.[3] Evidence shows that this can lead to singleness being frowned upon with single people subsequently feeling 'second class'.[4] However, there is a question that needs to be considered when seeking to understand the position of singleness within the church. Should we expect a greater proportion of married people within the church than in the wider community, and are the statistics simply reflecting this reality?

Social change

While investigating this matter, it became evident to me that the social change we have experienced has been a significant factor in how the church deals not only with marriage and families, but also with singleness. The social change in the British Isles since the 1960s, as described by Wilson, is similarly evident across the Western world. Comparable social change in the US is described by Köstenberger and Jones as occurring over the 'past few decades' prior to 2010.[5] In the research to which Andrews refers, he identifies similar social change across the Western world over the 'past four decades' prior to 2012.[6] This social change is also evident in Australia, corresponding with the time period when the change was occurring in other countries.[7] The NCLS report's statistics since the 1960s and 1970s reflects this change. The rate of marriage breakdown has increased as has the number of people who have never married. These factors have led to an increased proportion of single people in the population.

Wilson describes how most churches in the British Isles responded to this social change. They gave greater attention to promoting and supporting the traditional nuclear family unit. However, the same degree of support was not extended to single people.[8] In my experience, the approach to families and singleness in Australia today resembles that observed in the British Isles, as described by Wilson in 2005. In Australia, almost every church appears to have definite ideas about how to support marriage and families. However, their ideas about how, or if, single people are to be supported are less well defined. For example, Wilson observed that numerous sermons were preached on marriage and family values, but very few on the matter of singleness.[9]

Underlying issues

Approaching the topic of singleness within the broader topic of marriage, families and singleness, involves navigating a complex path through the issues involved. This chapter begins the discussion on the differences between the secular and biblical approaches. The following two chapters continue the discussion on the differences between, and the effects of, these approaches.

Köstenberger and Jones suggest that the abandonment of biblical foundations within society in relation to marriage and families has contributed to the social change since the 1960s and 1970s.[10] The pressure of this social change, exerted on marriages and families, has made it imperative for the church to respond. The response that the church chooses will have a flow-on effect for singleness. Therefore, dealing with singleness within the church today requires some understanding of the underlying issues facing marriage and families.

God's higher wisdom

The conversation and cases expounded by the secular social researchers examined by Andrews are, in my view, largely approached from a pro-family perspective. Over recent decades, attention has centred on marriages and families and on the consequences of the increasing rate of marriage and family breakdown.

For the church to develop a biblical understanding of the positions of singleness, marriage and families in society and in the church today, it is important to firstly consider how the secular view of these issues may impact on our understanding. What is the consequence of our society's understanding of these matters which has its roots in secular Greek philosophy?

There is a question which naturally arises. When the church considers this type of issue, or any other issue for that matter, should the findings of professionals and experts conducting secular-based research be accepted without question? In considering this, we need to remember that the interpretations they make may be based on, or influenced by, a non-biblical source, such as Greek philosophy.

When researchers are simply gathering physical data, it is quite appropriate for the church to respect the professionalism with which they do their research. However, when it comes to interpreting the data, the church may need to use more discernment in accepting their 'findings'. The education and training on which researchers base their conclusions and findings are not always in accord with biblical wisdom.

The Old Testament prophet Isaiah contrasts God's thoughts and His wisdom with that of human wisdom saying, '"for my thoughts are not your thoughts, neither are your ways my ways," declares the Lord. "As the heavens are higher than the earth, so are my ways higher than your ways and my thoughts than your thoughts"' (Isaiah 55:8-9). In the New Testament, we also find comparative statements about God's wisdom, for example, 'For the foolishness of God is wiser than human wisdom, and the weakness of God is stronger than human strength' (1 Corinthians 1:25). The church has the responsibility to look firstly to God's wisdom as revealed in His word. We need to measure the world's wisdom against what God has revealed to us, rather than unreservedly being directed by the wisdom of the world.

The omission of the cross

The message of the cross is central to God's plan for the whole of humanity and has been relevant throughout our history, as it is for the present and our future. For the secular world, this message is rejected as foolish. The apostle Paul says, 'For the message of the cross is foolishness to those who are perishing, but to us who are being saved it is the power of God' (1 Corinthians 1:18).

Another point of difference between secular and biblical approaches is the Holy Spirit's guidance. God's Spirit searches God's thoughts and teaches them to us (1 Corinthians 2:10-13). Paul says, 'The person without the Spirit does not accept the things that come from the Spirit of God, but considers them foolishness, and cannot understand them, because they are discerned only through the Spirit' (1 Corinthians 2:14).

The cross of Christ and discernment from the Holy Spirit are, at times, contributing factors to our understanding of the problems with which we are dealing. When they are contributing factors, we should expect to find that secular wisdom develops different solutions than the solutions inspired by God's wisdom. In gathering factual research information in which the cross of Christ and discernment from the Holy Spirit are not contributing factors, secular social research can provide useful information on society.

An illustration of what God says

Social researchers, Daniel Yankelovich in the US and Hugh Mackay in Australia, describe the changes in social values in the US and Australia following World War II, leading up to and including the 1970s and beyond. Both researchers trace similar trends during this time, including the inclination of individuals to 'look after number one' and 'do your own thing'.[11] Characteristic trends of that time, suggested by other researchers, include a 'culture of rights' and 'increasing materialism'.[12] Andrews comments on Mackay's (1997) *Generations: Baby Boomers, Their Parents and Their Children,* in which Mackay describes these trends as appearing to provide a framework for an ethical system in which the notion of restraint is absent.[13]

This observation by Mackay is perceptive, helping to provide the church with an insight into what has been happening, and continues to happen today, in society. We read in the biblical wisdom literature that, 'Where there is no revelation, the people cast off restraint' (Proverbs 29:18).

When a society is no longer receiving or listening to the revelations of God and His word, the expected consequence may be a society that is casting off restraint. This correlates with the outcome described by Mackay.

Thus, if God's word has been correctly understood, the observed social problems are a consequence of our society increasingly rejecting God's word. Therefore, the secular approach to dealing with the problems will ultimately not offer a solution.

One of the most obvious ramifications of the social change since the 1970s is the increased rate of family breakdown. A prominent secular way of thinking in addressing this problem is to suggest the need for stable families to build stable communities. The social research examined by Andrews illustrates this approach. The influence of the thought that 'families are the basic building blocks of society', with its roots in Greek philosophy, is evident, and is likely to have been in the forefront of the minds of many researchers when devising strategies to arrest this social trend. Families should, according to this secular line of thinking, be given a privileged and favoured position within society. However, from a biblical perspective, this is a reaction to a symptom and fails to address the cause. Restoring our relationship with God and our dependence on Him and His word is the response needed today to address the cause of social decline.

Effect of marriage on well-being

In biblical and secular approaches, factual research data may be interpreted differently. The influence of a secular interpretation can be seen in the following example.

Research during the past fifty years consistently indicates a higher level of health and well-being among married people than among those who are not married, as observed by Andrews in his study of wide-ranging social research.[14] This observation is consistent for many factors including mortality, suicides and accidents, morbidity, mental health, social isolation, employment and wealth.[15] One interpretation is to suggest that marriage has a 'protective effect' on people's well-being and happiness.[16]

In contrast to this secular view, the biblical view of protection and well-being is expressed in the Psalms: 'In peace I will lie down and sleep, for you alone, LORD, make me dwell in safety' (Psalm 4:8) and, 'I will fear no evil, for you are with me' (Psalm 23:4). The Old Testament prophet Isaiah makes a similar declaration, 'You keep him in perfect peace whose mind is stayed on you, because he trusts in you' (Isaiah 26:3 ESV). Revelations consistent with these passages are also made in the New Testament, firstly where Jesus describes himself as the 'good shepherd' who watches over us (John 10:11; see Psalm 23: 1–6), and further, where He declares, 'I have come that they may have life and have it to the full'(John 10:10).

The protection and well-being found through faith in Christ is available to all, which includes those who are single. It is only in the eternal things of the kingdom of God where we can truly find protection, peace and well-being in an environment where we are opposed by evil. Marriage is a temporal institution. It therefore does not seem feasible that marriage can provide protection where life has spiritual and eternal facets to its nature.

If marriage does not have a 'protective effect', as suggested by Andrews, what could explain the differences in well-being and happiness between those who are married and those who are not? A feasible explanation of the differences could, at least in part, be due to the consequences of negative cultural attitudes toward singleness. If secular philosophy's favouring of marriage and families creates a social environment where single people feel inconsequential and unvalued, this could have a negative impact on their well-being. Married people may experience a more accepting and supportive social environment. This could explain the suggested 'protective effect' of marriage. Those who are married may simply not have to endure the culturally devaluing attitudes to which single people are often subjected.

In my experience, an elevated view of marriage and childbearing can lead to them both being seen as culturally 'expected' or 'normal'. This may then have consequences in people's attitudes toward those who are single. Single people could be viewed as being outside the boundaries of what is expected as normal. Examples of this type of cultural expectation can be seen in both the Old and New Testaments. In the Old Testament, childlessness was viewed with shame or as a disgrace (Genesis 30:23). For example, Rachel, due to the negative cultural view of her situation, was distressed at not bearing any children (Genesis 30:23). In a further example, Hannah, Samuel's mother, had a similar experience (1 Samuel 1:11). The New Testament account of Elizabeth, the mother of John the Baptist, is again alike. She had been 'barren and … well advanced in years' when an angel of the Lord appeared to her husband and told him that she would bear a son (Luke 1:7 ESV). When she subsequently became pregnant, she spoke of her gratefulness saying, 'Thus the Lord has done for me in the days when He looked on me, to take away my reproach among people' (Luke 1:25 ESV).

Whatever factors are at work in our society affecting single people, the impacts are far-reaching. If even some of the attributed benefits of marriage could instead be attributed to the negative impacts of social attitudes toward single people, this would become an important factor for consideration and discussion. Discernment is needed in the church when considering secular social research which provides 'findings' on the way a community can best function.

Contrast of the secular approach

God took a rib from Adam's side and created the first woman, Eve (Genesis 2:21-22). She was taken out of man (Genesis 2:23) and God brought her to the man (Genesis 2:22). The word of God tells us that it is for this reason that a man and a woman are united in marriage and so become one flesh (Genesis 2:24). God's creation of woman from man is the basis for marriage and establishes marriage as a divine ordinance. Jesus alluded to this in His reply to a question from some Pharisees about divorce (Matthew 19:4-6). God's creation of the man and woman is the authority that Jesus uses to establish that it is God who joins the man and his wife together in their marriage. Jesus said it had been this way from the beginning and, therefore, what God had joined together no-one should separate (Mark 10:6-9; Matthew 19:4-6; Genesis 2:24).

Our secular society seeks other ways to explain the basis of marriage. This is illustrated in Andrews' explanation:

> Christian views about marriage were a fusion of the earlier Greek philosophy and later theological perspectives. This is why attempts to label marriage as simply a religious issue are misplaced. Religions recognise and bless marriage, but they did not invent it.[17]

With this view that marriage is not God's 'invention', it follows that it must be a human invention. Changes to the form of marriage and families would, therefore, simply be a re-invention to create something more appropriate for today. Andrews gives an example of what could be a consequence of this line of thinking. A 'prevalent' view in the US is that marriage and families are in transition to a more diverse and fluid form.[18]

This secular view and the biblical view lead in different directions. Each would inevitably result in different outcomes if applied to addressing the impacts of the social change.

Social philosophies

Köstenberger and Jones[19], Andrews[20] and Wilson[21] each describe secular philosophies that have influenced the social change since 1960, including social philosophies aimed at deconstructing traditional marriage and family. Andrews and Wilson both identify the social philosophies of postmodernism and deconstructionism originating in the 1960s.[22] They suggest that these philosophies, and particularly the aspects advocated by French critics Michel Foucault and Jacques Derrida, are among the cultural influences most disruptive to previously held beliefs on marriage and families.[23] In the US, Köstenberger and Jones describe libertarian ideology as having a significant influence on social morality.[24] They consequently suggest it forms a competing morality to the West's Judeo-Christian heritage with detrimental consequences for marriages and families.[25]

Andrews also discusses the views presented by social scientist Edmund Leach in the 1967 Reith Lectures, *A Runaway World?* Leach suggests that the nuclear family is not a good basis for society. His view is that children should be raised in larger domestic community groups similar to the Israeli kibbutz or a Chinese commune.[26]

Wilson describes the philosophy of North American scholars Libby and Whitehurst who, in 1977, suggested changes to the institution of marriage. They viewed monogamy as an outdated ideal and suggested cohabitation, open marriages and group marriages as alternatives.[27]

Spectrum of secular ideas

Ideas advocating the deconstruction of traditional marriage and families lie at one end of a spectrum. The spectrum displays the range of secular ideas relating to the value of marriage and families within society. Ideas on the 'deconstruction' of marriage and families end of the spectrum are closely linked with the social change in our society since the 1960s and 1970s. One of the most evident problems associated with this social change has been the increase in marriage and family breakdown.

The devastating consequences of the increased breakdown of marriages and families have required a response. A secular response has come from the opposite end of the spectrum. It assigns favouritism and exalts the position of the traditional forms of marriage and families within society. Concepts of this 'favouritism' of marriage and families end of the spectrum maintain, for example, that families are the foundation on which society is built[28] and that they are the building blocks of society.[29] It is suggested that the health of the family unit is the barometer of the health of the society[30] and, thus, that the disintegration of the family is a threat to the cohesion of society as a whole.[31] Aristotle's philosophy relating to the necessity of families for *eudaimonia* comes from this 'favouritism' of families end of the spectrum. A reflection of Aristotle's philosophy is seen in the conclusion drawn by Andrews from his examination of secular social research, when he writes, 'a healthy marriage is the best source of physical and mental health, emotional stability and prosperity for adults and children. It is also the best bet for attaining happiness and fulfilment'.[32]

Figure 2.1: The spectrum of secular ideas on the value of marriage and families within society

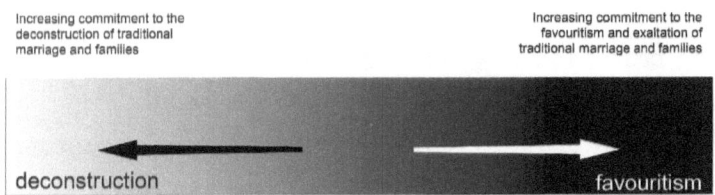

Further results of the social research examined by Andrews also illustrate the 'favouritism' of marriage and families end of the spectrum. Andrews concludes from the secular social research he examined that a stable marriage between a man and a woman is the greatest hope of humanity.[33] A natural consequence of this perspective would be to assume that the greatest threat for humanity would come from the decay and breakdown of marriage and families.[34] From this viewpoint, the other end of the spectrum, the 'deconstruction' of marriage and the family, represents the greatest threat.

It is straightforward reasoning then, viewing the situation from the 'favouritism' of marriage and families end of the spectrum, to suggest that giving marriage and families the most privileged and exalted position within society would be for the benefit of society as a whole. However, this is not a biblical approach. A stable marriage between a man and a woman is good within itself; however, it does not represent the greatest hope of humanity.

Viewed from a biblical perspective, the struggle with slavery to sin presents the greatest threat to humanity (Romans 6:6; Romans 6:16). Jesus proved that He had the power over sin and death, and power on earth to forgive a person's sin, by his resurrection from the dead. In this is found the greatest hope of humanity. From a biblical perspective, the greatest hope of humanity is found in Christ, the 'last Adam', rather than in marriage, the pattern of the 'first Adam'.[35]

Problems at both ends

Each end of this spectrum, of secular ideas on the value of marriage and families, creates its own social and spiritual problems. On the 'deconstruction' of marriage and families end of the spectrum, the breakdown of marriage and families is the most visible effect. On the other end, the 'favouritism' of marriage and families end of the spectrum, the effect is the undue exalting of marriage and families and the devaluing and marginalising of those who are single or from broken marriages or broken families.

The ideas advocating deconstruction of marriage and families have clearly had destructive consequences for our society and they do not reflect God's word. Marriage is ordained by God (Mark 10:6–9; Matthew 19:4–6; Genesis 2:24). Families are also instituted by God (see Ephesians 6:1–4; 1 Timothy 3:4; 1 Timothy 5:8). It is dismissive of God and His ways to try to deconstruct traditional marriage and families as has been endorsed by some social philosophies. In my experience, it is not uncommon within the church to therefore conclude that the other end of the spectrum, the 'favouritism' of marriage and families, must be the biblical response. However, this end of the spectrum is equally dismissive of God and His ways.

Our materialistic and naturalistic secular society, that has rejected Christ (John 1:11), lacks the spiritual resources to fully deal with social problems that have a spiritual cause.

The breakdown of marriage and families is a symptom of the social change. The cause is related to society's rejection of God's ways. Favouring and exalting marriage and families are a reaction to the symptom but fail to deal with the cause. God shows no favouritism (Romans 2:11); therefore, showing favouritism to marriage and families by affording them a higher social position is not God's way.

Within our society, if the position of marriage and families is to be elevated, an inevitable consequence is to devalue those who are single or childless or from broken marriages or families above whom they are to be elevated. Any group within society cannot have their position raised relative to society as a whole, without other groups within that society having their position relatively lowered.

On the 'favouritism' end of the spectrum, secular social philosophies present numerous ideas that advocate for the undue elevation of the importance and position of marriages and families within society. The impact that these ideas have on singleness may be unintentional, but they are real. For example, if families are perceived to be the foundation and building blocks of society, of what value are those who are single or childless or from broken families? Are they inconsequential or of less importance to society? If the greatest hope of humanity is thought to be marriage, what of those who are single? Are they inherently of less value because they are not married? If families are envisaged as holding nations together and if families are adjudged to be necessary for fulfilment in life, are those who are single or from broken families less important, an underclass in society? The spectrum of ideas on the value of marriage and families within society, as discussed above, is a spectrum of secular ideas. The response to the social change that offers favouritism for, and the exalting of, marriage and families, does not deal with the cause of the problem and is not a biblical response (1 Corinthians 12:25).

Starting at the centre

The starting point of a faith response to the social change experienced over the past fifty or sixty years is at the centre of the secular spectrum. In this response, neither the 'deconstruction' of marriage and the family nor 'favouritism' and the exalting of marriage and the family, the two ends of the secular spectrum, are embraced.

Figure 2.2: Dealing with sin through faith in Christ, and trusting in God's word, adds a different dimension to finding a solution to the social problems we are facing

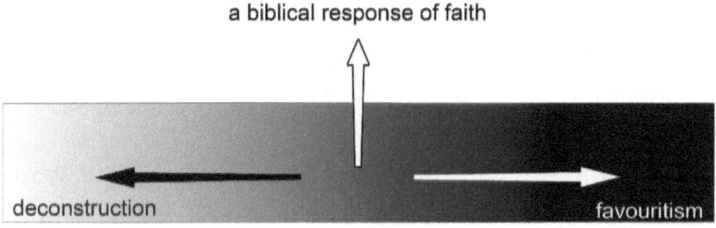

From this starting point, all matters relating to marriage, family and singleness can be dealt with through Jesus and His word, by faith, without the influence of unhelpful secular ideas (see 2 Peter 1:3; 2 Timothy 3:16).

God, in His wisdom, tells us that 'righteousness exalts a nation' (Proverbs 14:34). He also gives us insight into why a nation will be exalted by righteousness. God's word speaks of Christ saying, 'all things have been created by him and for him. He is before all things, and in him all things hold together' (Colossians 1:16–17). We also read that, 'The Son is the radiance of God's glory and the exact representation of his being, sustaining all things by his powerful word' (Hebrews 1:3). A society that increasingly rejects Christ and His word will not be sustained and held together in the same way as would a society faithful to Christ and His word. It is reasonable to think that 'all things' held together and sustained by Jesus and His powerful word include individuals, marriages, families, communities and nations.

The general movement away from trust in God by our society should be expected to be a factor in the social problems experienced today. The response needed within our society is reconciliation with God and restored dependence on Him and His word to begin addressing the cause of the social decline.

The wisdom of God, found in Jesus Christ and His word, adds a different dimension to the search for a solution to the social problems being faced. The social decline of recent decades is a problem caused by sin that will not be overcome by secular reasoning. In a secular response, our own human efforts and wisdom are relied upon, whereas a biblical response depends on the wisdom of Jesus Christ and His word, through the guidance of the Holy Spirit, and is a response of faith.

The church — precious to God

The church are those who hear and obey God's word (Luke 8:21; John 14:21) and they are precious to Him. God's plan is for the reconciliation of humanity to himself through His Son. This entails the formation of the church on earth in these last days. The culmination of His plan for humanity is for the church to be prepared in righteousness (Revelation 19:8) as a bride for the Lamb.

Through the prophets, God speaks about His people in compassionate ways. For example, He says, 'see, I have engraved you on the palms of my hands' (Isaiah 49:16); 'whoever touches you touches the apple of his eye' (Zechariah 2:8); and 'Come, I will show you the bride ... of the Lamb' (Revelation 21:9).

God chooses to act in the world through the church today and calls His people 'a chosen people, a royal priesthood, a holy nation, God's special possession' (1 Peter 2:9).

Enemies of God and His people

Through the cross, God's enemies suffered defeat in their direct opposition to God's Son (Colossians 2:15). Therefore, it is reasonable to think that their opposition would next be directed against the people of God. God's people are precious to Him and through them He chooses to achieve His purpose in the world.

In God's word, all that is opposed to God is collectively referred to as 'the world'. Erickson describes the term 'the world', when used in this context, as the antithesis of the kingdom of God.[36] He refers to its enmity, hostility and opposition directed against Christ and those who belong to Him by both human and spiritual elements.

God's word confirms that the world shows opposition to God's people. We read that, 'If you belonged to the world, it would love you as its own. As it is, you do not belong to the world, but I have chosen you out of the world. That is why the world hates you' (John 15:18–19). God's word also describes 'the prince of this world' (John 16:11) as 'the accuser of our brothers ... who accuses them day and night before our God' (Revelation 12:10 ESV). Again it is evident that those who have faith in Christ are opposed by Satan.

The well-being of the church

God's word tells us that, through our faith in Jesus Christ, we are equipped to overcome the world's opposition, saying, 'for everyone born of God overcomes the world. This is the victory that has overcome the world, even our faith' (1 John 5:4).

The way that we respond to today's social pressures on marriage and family has implications for the well-being of the church. Before the church embraces any interpretations of secular social research, that research, and the principles on which it is based, should be measured against the wisdom of God, as found in His word.

Guarding against the influence of unhelpful secular ideas is like guarding the back door through which the church could be invaded and undermined if we do not take care to act in faith. Everyone is created by God for a purpose; therefore, everyone's contribution is important in God's plan for the whole of humanity. Everyone can find life to the full in Jesus Christ (John 10:10), whether married or single, with the only true hope of humanity to be found in Him.

Building on the rock

The parable told by Jesus about the wise builder and the foolish builder illustrates the biblical teaching on the profitable guidance of God's word for building any stable association or relationship, including building a nation. Jesus gave direction to His people, including every individual among them, saying:

> Therefore, everyone who hears these words of mine and puts them into practice is like a wise man who built his house on the rock. The rain came down, the stream rose, and the winds blew and beat against that house; yet it did not fall because it had its foundation on the rock. But everyone who hears these words of mine and does not put them into practice is like a foolish man who built his house on sand ... and it fell with a great crash. (Matthew 7:24–27)

A storm is raging today, in the form of social and cultural change, against those in the church. Jesus' parable of the wise and foolish builders (Matthew 7:24–27) reassures us that those who hear and put into practice His word will withstand the storm (Matthew 7:25). The storm will still rage against the church, with opposition, criticism and ridicule from the world. However, those within the church who faithfully follow Christ will prevail. This will not be from our own human efforts, but through the hand of God acting to fulfil His promise. God expresses no favouritism. Through faith, single people, no less than those who are married and with families, are included in His purpose.

Chapter 3

Foundations

Chapter 2 contrasted the secular and biblical approaches, in general terms, to issues that have emerged in response to the social change of recent decades in respect to marriage, families and singleness. This chapter continues to reflect on these approaches by looking at more specific elements of both the change and the response. The discussion in this chapter continues to examine the way in which the secular approach is a reaction to the symptoms, while the biblical approach deals with the cause. How matters relating to marriage and families are approached will inevitably affect how singleness is viewed.

Defining love

God is love (1 John 4:8), with love being an important concept in the kingdom of God. Love is referred to in the current chapter's discussion and in the chapters that follow.

However, clarification is needed to comprehend what is meant in the original biblical text when speaking of love, to avoid any misunderstanding.

In the original New Testament text, three different Greek words are used for the one English word 'love'. The Greek word *agape* describes the self-sacrificing love demonstrated to us by Christ, and which we can also have for others. In Ephesians 5:25, Paul writes of this type of love as the love that husbands should have for their wives. It is also clear that God wants us to share great love within our families and to care for them (1 Timothy 5:8). The Greek word *storge* describes family love, such as that between parents and children. The Greek word *phileo* describes the love for someone considered a friend with whom we have a bond of friendship. A fourth Greek word for love, *eros*, describes romantic, passionate, sexual love. It is not found in the New Testament text; however, it helps provide an understanding of the range of words and meaning in the Greek language for the English word 'love'.[1]

Factors influencing change

Wilson, Andrews, and Köstenberger and Jones identify the changing view of social morality that was shaping Western society in the 1960s and 1970s. Technology, political factors and social philosophies all influenced the revision of social norms. Gender relations were changing, with influencing factors including the introduction of no-fault divorce in the UK in 1969 and in Australia in 1975; moves toward increased educational and occupational opportunities for women; and the ready availability of contraception.[2]

The social philosophies serving as the catalyst for social change in the 1960s and 1970s were often characterised by their contribution to the deconstruction of traditional Judeo-Christian concepts of marriage and family.[3] These philosophies were set against the belief that it is God who ordained the pattern for marriage (Genesis 2:24), and who gives the parenting mandate.[4] Embedded within the social change was society's inclination to replace God's wisdom and our traditional Judeo-Christian heritage with alternative secular social ideas.

Two distinct approaches

Some sought to defend society against the forces committed to the deconstruction of marriage and the family and to address the increased rate of marriage and family breakdown. Their actions, influenced by secular wisdom, have led to marriages and families being assigned a higher position within society than would otherwise have occurred. However, in this approach, the cause of the social decline is not addressed. Biblical wisdom addresses the problems being faced in a different way.

A biblical approach

A biblical response to the social change would begin by restoring the broken foundations on which our society has chosen to build. Over past decades, changes to our laws and social morality have increasingly been based on what seems right in our own eyes. However, historically, the law and social morality of Australian society have been based on our Judeo–Christian heritage and values, thus being centred on God's word.[5]

Unlike the secular approach, a biblical approach does not exalt one group above another, but rather exalts Christ and His word. A biblical approach recognises the importance of our spiritual condition. The internal matters of the heart and mind are given greater consideration than our position within society.

The word of God likens those who belong to God's family to a body with many parts. The value of each part within the body does not depend on the function we have within the body. Our standing comes from being 'in Christ'; therefore, each part should have equal concern for every other part (1 Corinthians 12:25; Galatians 3:26–28). Those who are married and have children are important in God's family, as are those who are single or from broken marriages or broken families. The reason for this is that our importance comes from being 'in Christ' and not from being 'in marriage' or 'in family'.

A secular approach

Our secular society has rejected Christ, and thus approaches problems caused by sin differently to a biblical approach. This is illustrated in the previously discussed spectrum of secular ideas. At the 'favouritism' of marriage and families end of the spectrum is the suggestion that marriage and families are not only an important part of society but that they are the most important part. The implication is that those who are single or from broken marriages or broken families are of less importance. This creates a division whereas, for those who are 'in Christ', no division exists.

This secular thinking is reflected in Australia's culture. The discussion in Chapter 2 provides the example of a conclusion drawn from secular research. It suggests that marriage is not merely a beneficial relationship that gives hope but that it is the greatest hope of humanity.[6] A further example is the way in which families are celebrated nationally. National Families Week is supported by Australia's government and is described as 'Australia's annual celebration of families'.[7] The event's information page on its website includes a description of families not only as important in building a community but states that 'families are the most important building blocks of communities, societies and nations'.[8] It naturally follows, from this viewpoint, that those who are single or childless or from broken families are of less importance in building a society than those who are married with children.

A further example is the way in which the concept of a cornerstone is used to describe families. A cornerstone is the first and most important stone in the foundation of a building, with everything in the building set in reference to it. Some social commentary within Australia suggests that families are not only important within the order of society, but that they are the cornerstone of society.[9]

These ideas come from one end of the spectrum of secular ideas on the value of marriage and family in society. The view of marriage and families as the most important part of society can inadvertently be devaluing to those who are not married or childless or from broken marriages or broken families.

Detrimental to the church

The secular idea of families being the most important part of society is incompatible with the message God has entrusted to the church. Within the context of Jesus' parable of the wise and foolish builders (Matthew 7:24–27), any secular concept that is allowed to influence the church is like the church building on a foundation of sand. We are immersed in a culture that offers the solution to our social problems through the privileging of marriage and families. For those within God's family, the enticement is to support the building of society in this way. However, it is not the way of faith, and ultimately it would be ineffective.

Within the current discussions, the most significant problem being addressed in society is the breakdown of marriages and families. Stable and happy marriages and families are, at times, held up as an ideal on which our future depends and in which we can place our hope.[10] Incentives and encouragement are offered to work toward the ideal through our own efforts and hard work. However, in the secular approach, the solution does not encompass the need to deal with sin and rebellion against God. A biblical approach begins in reconciliation with God through repentance and forgiveness of sin and is based on the cross of Christ. This means that everyone, whether married or single, is in the same position before God.

Marriage and families replacing Christ

The social change experienced since the 1960s and 1970s is a challenge to both the church and wider society. Our entire society has had to deal with the consequences of moral decline. From a biblical perspective, the social problems have a moral and spiritual cause and the only true and righteous way to address them would be for our society to again become a God-fearing society and place our faith and hope in Christ (Psalm 33:12; Colossians 1:16-17; Hebrews 1:3). However, to a fallen world, this is unpalatable (see John 3:19). Having rejected Christ, the world will naturally try to place its faith and hope in something else. In relation to improving society, the 'something else' to replace Christ is often the family. This is illustrated in the following examples.

Building blocks of society

Aristotle viewed families as the 'basic building blocks' of the whole of society.[11] This forms a neat ideology for some people today. However, the implication inevitably attached to this philosophy, is that those who are single, or childless, or from broken marriages or broken families, are of less consequence in the building of society than those who are married with children.

By honouring God and His righteous ways, a nation will be blessed and exalted (Psalm 33:12, Proverbs 14:34). Every individual is called to this righteousness (Acts 17:30, Ephesians 4:24), and the righteousness of every individual can contribute to building the nation according to God's plan and purpose. Each individual person is responsible and accountable to God to walk in righteousness (2 Corinthians 5:10). This applies equally to individuals who are single as it does to those who are married.

A practical reality is that those who are single contribute to building a society in the same way as those who are married and have children. Jesus, as a single person, provides the perfect example. Today the contribution made by Jesus to the building of society continues to be relevant and needed, just as it always has been. However, our secular society rejects Jesus, and its chosen philosophy rejects His contribution. Yet the contribution by Jesus is the only one dealing with the cause of social problems associated with the social change.

The apostle Paul was single, and he was the most prolific contributor to the writing of the New Testament. In the two millennium since the time of Paul, many single people have also made significant contributions to the building of society. A question arises here of whether Aristotle's philosophy is a sound and reasonable philosophy or whether it is simply a convenient philosophy.

Foundational institution of society

Other ideas are used to justify the assignment of a higher place to marriage and families within society or the church than they would otherwise have. An example is the view that our natural families are the primary and most fundamental unit of society.[12]

The most foundational relationship we can have in any part of life is our individual relationship with God, our creator (see Luke 14:26). Before the world was created, God chose us for this relationship with Him in Christ (Ephesians 1:4). Through this most foundational of relationships, we are given the right to become the children of God (John 1:12). Therefore, our position in God's family is more basic and foundational than our position in any other institution, including that of marriage or family.

We read in God's word that 'God placed all things under his feet and appointed him to be head over everything for the church' (Ephesians 1:22). It is Christ who is the head of the church (Colossians 1:18), which is His body (Ephesians 1:23), and it is the family of God through whom God chooses to work in the world. It is reasonable to believe, then, that in both time and importance, the family of God is the most foundational institution that can possibly exist within our physical society.

Israel was God's chosen nation of the Old Testament. For the people of Israel, marriage and family were a central part of inheriting the promises God made to them as Abraham's descendants. However, a further unveiling of God's purpose for humanity was revealed with the advent of Christ into the world. In relation to families, Jesus said, 'My mother and my brothers are those who hear God's word and put it into practice' (Luke 8:21). In the new community that Jesus came to establish, He placed the spiritual and the eternal before and above the physical and the temporal. In the unfolding of His purpose for all of humanity, He placed the family of God before and above our natural families. He turned our focus toward His family of faith in inheriting God's promises and away from the central focus on natural families.

Within contemporary society, the secular concept of natural families as the primary and most foundational institution of the community serves to justify the re-establishment of the centrality of the natural family. It is dismissive of what Jesus came to establish. It is a step backward, not forward, in dealing with the cause of the problems associated with the social change, because it is only in Christ and His ways that problems caused by sin can be addressed.

Joseph H. Hellerman makes a similar point in his article: 'Our priorities are off when family is more important than church'.[13] He suggests that a return to early Christian relational priorities of seeing God's family as our primary family is important to improve the health of the Western church and to advance personal spiritual growth. He also suggests that this approach will lead to less privileging of marriages and families and a stronger theology of singleness and celibacy. He is not taking an anti-family stance, nor is he arguing that the Bible is anti-family. Rather, he is saying that keeping a correct biblical perspective on families will result in a better outcome for marriages and families, as well as for the church as a whole.

Foundation of society

Secular social research's perspective, as presented by Andrews, is of the family being viewed as the bedrock, or foundation, on which a successful society is built.[14] Three general points should be made regarding this perspective.

Firstly, it is noted that the greatest concern resulting from the social change since the 1960s and 1970s has been the increased breakdown of marriages and families. This, in itself, gives sufficient reason to suggest that families are unsuitable as the foundation of society as they are susceptible to breaking down. Marriage and families are good within themselves; however, society needs a more stable foundation than the one that families can provide. God's word tells us that Jesus' kingdom that we are inheriting cannot be shaken (Hebrews 12:28). Christ and His word are a stable foundation on which a society can be built (Hebrews 1:3). In recent decades our society has built on foundations other than Christ. Only through Christ can the cause of the problems associated with the social change be addressed.

Secondly, the basis for how to build a society was established by God at the creation of the world. Consider God's instruction to the first creatures created. On the fifth day of creation, God spoke and created the creatures of the sea and the birds of the air (Genesis 1:20–21; Psalm 33:9). Following this, God blessed them and said, 'Be fruitful and increase in number' (Genesis 1:22). A question to ponder here is whether this was a verbal instruction from God that the creatures of the sea and the birds of the air comprehended and carried out? It is possible that the meaning of this verse, describing what God said on the fifth day of creation, is that God created within them a desire and instinct for reproduction to ensure the survival of their species.[15]

On the following day, the sixth day of creation, God created mankind and blessed them and said, 'Be fruitful and increase in number' (Genesis 1:28). It is also possible that a part of the meaning of this verse, describing what God said to the man and the woman, is that He created within them a reproductive desire to ensure the survival of mankind. Whether it is at this time or another that a reproductive desire was placed in the hearts and minds of humanity, it is reasonable to think that it was given to us by God to ensure the survival of mankind.

God has also placed His law in the hearts and minds of His people (Jeremiah 31:33). Even those who do not otherwise know God's law have within them an awareness of God's law (Romans 2:14–15). Our conscience is a testimony to this.

Jesus gave a summary of God's law by saying, 'Love the Lord your God with all your heart and with all your soul and with all your mind.' This is the first and greatest commandment. And the second is: 'Love your neighbour as yourself.' All that is said in the Law and Prophets are encapsulated in these two commandments (Matthew 22:37–40).

The law that God has placed within us, even within those who do not otherwise know God's law, therefore has love as its basis (Romans 13:10). The love referred to here is *agape* love. The apostle John tells us about love saying, 'And this is love: that we walk in obedience to his commands' (2 John 1:6). The intended outworking of the love that God has placed within us fulfils His moral law[16] and so builds moral character. God has given all of humanity an awareness of, and potential for, a loving and moral character, based on His law (Matthew 22:37–40). This, then, gives us the basis on which to build our relationships, and on which to build our society, even for those who do not otherwise know God's law (Romans 2:14–15).

In the context of our discussion on marriage, families and singleness, it is significant to note that this potential for a loving and moral character within us was intended by God to be connected and subject to the person of Jesus Christ. We read in God's word, 'All things were created through him and for him' (Colossians 1:16). This potential for a loving and moral character will only be in harmony with the purpose for which it was created when it is connected with Jesus. It is in Christ that all things are held together (Colossians 1:17). When our society is not connected or subject to the person of Jesus Christ, our society does not fully function in the way it was created to function.

A properly functioning society is built on the loving and moral character, based on God's law, placed in our hearts and minds. It is this character, rather than marriage or families or the reproductive desire that God has placed within us that enables society to function in the political, social and spiritual way that is intended.

This loving and moral character can be distorted by sin. Our conscience can even become 'seared as with a hot iron' (1 Timothy 4:2). The social change we have experienced since the 1960s and 1970s has seen a distortion of that which God placed within the hearts and minds of people in our society. Both the law of God and the reproductive desire that God placed in people's hearts and minds have been distorted. Our society is now built more on what naturally emerges from our sinful human hearts than on what comes from the heart of God.

When our hearts and minds, in which the law of God has been placed, are connected and subject to Jesus Christ, He will begin to produce righteousness within us. God tells us that it is righteousness that exalts a nation (Proverbs 14:34). Although marriage and families are important for the order of society, not all marriages and families are righteous in God's sight. Not all people who are righteous in God's sight are married with children.

Marriage, as an institution, enables our reproductive desire to be expressed in a loving and moral way. Marriages and families also have social and spiritual benefits. However, they are not the whole story of society. It is the righteousness of a marriage and family that contributes to society more than the family's structure. This point is discussed further in Chapter 4. In addition, the righteousness of people who are not married can contribute to society in the same way as the righteousness of those who are married.

This leads to the third point, that although having a spouse and children has an important part to play within society, marriage and family do not comprise all of society. It is also questionable whether the institution of the family is the most important aspect of society. Jesus' family was important to Him. However, when He said that His family were those who heard God's words and put them into practice (Luke 8:21), He was not considering the natural family to be the most significant part of society.

Not all people are called to marriage and having children. Jesus is our example to verify this. Therefore, the secular philosophy of the family being viewed as the foundation of society is narrowly focused and fails to take into consideration all of society. Or if it is considering all of society, it implies that those who are single and without children or from broken marriages or broken families are of less consequence to society than those who are married with children. Marriage and families are not the foundation of society because they require their own foundation, as does all of creation, with that foundation being Christ and His word (1 Corinthians 3:11; Matthew 7:24–25).

A flourishing society

Aristotle viewed the family as necessary for *eudaimonia*[17] and his philosophy continues to influence today's thinking about society.[18] However, the biblical view is that Jesus offers fulfilment and abundance in life. He says, 'I have come that they may have life and have it to the full' (John 10:10). The apostle Peter also assures us of the sufficiency of Christ saying, 'His divine power has given us everything we need for a godly life through our knowledge of him' (2 Peter 1:3). This is true for everyone within God's family, whether married or single, because everyone is equal before God (1 Corinthians 12:25–27).

Holding nations together

Understanding the characteristics of Christ's relationship to creation helps to establish a biblical approach for dealing with the impacts of social change. God's word says about Jesus, '… in him all things hold together' (Colossians 1:17). It also says that He is 'the radiance of God's glory … sustaining all things by his powerful word' (Hebrews 1:3). Ultimately, it is through Christ and His word that nations are sustained and held together.

In the secular concept that families are what sustains and holds nations together, Christ and His word are replaced by the family. The views attributed to historian Arnold Toynbee, for example, have been used to popularise this concept. He is quoted as saying, 'nations rise and fall with the health of its families'.[19]

From a biblical viewpoint, a society that rejects Christ will not function coherently in the way in which God created it to function. In a society that rejects the powerful word of God, it should not be unexpected that social decline will follow.

The greatest hope of humanity

The final idea mentioned here is a conclusion derived from secular social research on marriage within society. Andrews provides this perspective, saying that a stable marriage of a man and a woman is the greatest hope of humanity.[20] In contrast, the biblical view is that only through the forgiveness of our sin and reconciliation with God can we experience the fullness of life and find true hope for humanity. This hope, which is in Christ, is for all people, irrespective of whether they are married and have children or are single or without children or from broken marriages or broken families.

Flow-on effect

The secular concepts discussed above are from our society's reaction to the symptoms of the social change. However, exalting the position of marriage and families within society will ultimately be ineffective in dealing with problems caused by sin. Only in exalting Christ and His word will the cause of these problems be addressed.

Another reason for identifying these concepts is their connection with the way in which singleness is viewed. When Christ and His word are honoured and exalted as the means through which society is held together and sustained, the righteous contribution and faith of all people is important. When Christ is acknowledged as the fulfilment and greatest hope of society, all people who are born of the Spirit of God will rejoice in Christ together in unity. When our relationship with God's family is of primary importance, no distinction will be made between those who are married with children and those who are single or without children or from broken marriages or broken families, because everyone is equal before God (1 Corinthians 12:25–27).

The connection and flow-on effect between the approach to marriage and families and the view of singleness potentially leads to unintended outcomes. People may take action to elevate the position of marriage and families in a sincere attempt to overcome, or balance out, the social pressures being experienced. However, in so doing, they may unintentionally cause detriment to those who are single. This can happen within the church. The solution to some issues faced by single people within the church could simply be for the church to be aware of this blind spot of the inadvertent flow-on effect the approach to marriage and families can have on those who are not married or without children and those from broken marriages or broken families.

Love within families

The pressures on marriages and families that cause their breakdown are the result of what is happening internally within the marriage or family. It is only what we allow to influence us within our marriages and families that has an effect. Strategies favouring marriage and families and exalting them in society only act in ways external to the marriage and family. It needs to be recognised that raising the status of marriage and families within society does not correspond to helping overcome internal spiritual problems within a family.

The love of which Jesus spoke when saying, 'Greater love has no one than this, that someone lay down his life for his friends' (John 15:13 ESV) is the same love that we can have for others as we become like Him. Paul specifically mentioned this kind of *agape* love within marriage when He said, 'Husbands, love your wives, just as Christ loved the church and gave himself up for her' (Ephesians 5:25). Love is an important aspect of family relationships. The godly *agape* love can be experienced within a family, in the same way as the *storge* type of family love. Love is also an important part of relationships within God's family, because God is *agape* love (1 John 4:8).

The importance of how love is shared within marriage or family relationships is the same whether the family has a high or low standing in society. This internal love of God and obedience to His word is necessary within a marriage and a family to avoid the detrimental influence of social change. However, the secular reaction of assigning marriage and families a higher position within society does not bring about the needed result.

The converse situation

The interconnection of factors in the approach to marriage, families and singleness can also be seen when considering the converse situation. In the early church, a situation arose in which singleness was ascribed a higher position within society than that of marriage. The apostle Paul described a situation in which some people over-estimated the importance of singleness and began to forbid people to marry (1 Timothy 4:1–3). By forbidding marriage, the over-estimating of the value of singleness was leading to the ultimate devaluing of marriage and families. In his criticism of the position held by these people, Paul was not diminishing the importance of singleness, with Paul being single himself. Instead, he was critical of those who had abandoned faith rather than following the truths of faith and good teaching (1 Timothy 4:6).

Detrimental to marriage and families

Secular ideas can potentially influence the church's approach to singleness and bring adverse consequences. However, the influence of secular philosophy within the church can also have detrimental consequences for marriages and families.

God's word recognises that enemies exist who would like to undermine society and the church. However, Jesus defeated these enemies on the cross (Colossians 2:15; 1 John 5:4). When marriage and families are upheld as the most important part of society or the church, they become a target for undermining. Although Jesus defeated the enemies on the cross (Colossians 2:15), the victory needs to be applied by faith (1 John 5:4). Where faith in marriage or family has replaced faith in Christ as the most important hope of society, the victory ensured by faith over these enemies is lost (see also Matthew 7:24–27).

If families became our hope of fulfilment and flourishing within the church, the enemies of the church, in their quest to see the church diminish, would be encouraged to undermine families. If, through the influence of secular ideas, our hope lay in families to hold society together, then families would become the target of enemies wanting society to fall apart. If marriage became our greatest hope within the church, the enemies who wanted to remove hope from the church would be encouraged to undermine marriages. If families are upheld as the foundation of society, then families would become the target of enemies wanting society to collapse.

Secular philosophy may appear, at first, to be supporting marriages and families, but ultimately those ideas will only add to the problems being faced. The social change of recent decades relates to our society moving away from trusting in God and His ways: it is only through the message of the cross that the subsequent problems will be effectively addressed.

Chapter 4

A Broader View

The church needs to carefully consider how it evaluates secular philosophy in the light of the words spoken by Jesus. He tells us that His kingdom is not of this world (John 18:36), rather it is eternal, whereas the physical world is temporal. Western society adheres largely to a mindset and world view of materialism and naturalism. In our society, the physical world is of greatest significance and eternal aspects of life are minimised or dismissed.

This chapter takes a broader view of marriage, family and singleness, both in the church and in society. It further contrasts the differences between a secular approach and a biblical approach. Discussing the structure of marriages and families will help highlight the incompatibility between the secular approach and the biblical approach in dealing with the implications of social change.

Elements of marriage

God's word tells us that all authority within a society exists because it has been established by God (Romans 13:1; John 19:11). Ultimately, the positions and roles we have within the order of society all come under God's authority. Marriage, for example, is a part of how society is ordered and was ordained by God at the beginning of creation. Jesus detailed the origin of marriage in His explanation to some Pharisees, saying:

> Haven't you read ... at the beginning the Creator made them male and female ... For this reason a man will leave his father and mother and be united with his wife and the two will become one flesh. So they are no longer two but one flesh. Therefore what God has joined together, let man not separate. (Matthew 19:4–6)

Three elements of God's order for marriage in this explanation are that marriage is between a man and a woman; that the man and woman are joined together by God; and that marriage is for life. The traditional view of marriage within Western society almost exclusively embraced these three elements.

Over the past fifty or sixty years, social norms in relation to marriage have been modified. Secular society now understands marriage as incorporating a broader spectrum of ideas than those previously held. Within contemporary society, other unions such as de facto marriage (common-law marriage), divorce and re-marriage, and same sex marriage have become normalised.

Traditionally, marriage in Western society was seen in terms of God joining a husband and his wife together. Therefore, marriage was usually performed by a minister of religion. Now, however, more civil marriage ceremonies are occurring. Statistical records show that 97% of marriages in Australia were performed by ministers of religion in 1902 whereas, in 2020, civil celebrants performed the ceremony in 80% of marriages.[1]

Figure 4.1: Marriages performed in Australia by ministers of religion compared to those performed by civil celebrants[2]

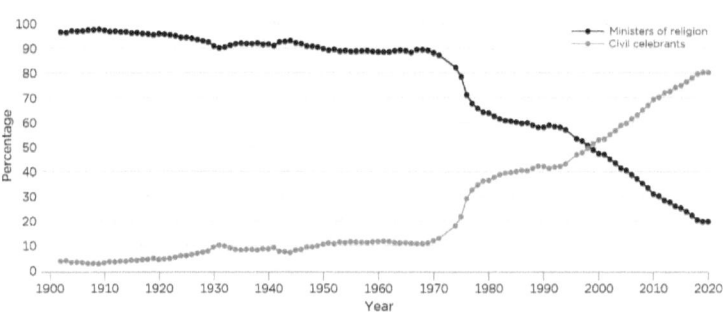

God ordained marriage; however, defining a union as a marriage is not sufficient for it to take on the righteousness of God. Our society's choice to move away from God and His word is now being incorporated into how marriage is defined. Care and discernment are therefore needed within the church to avoid being influenced by the secular approach to marriage and families, in a general sense, within society. Otherwise, the result could be the upholding within the church of some marriage arrangements that are not consistent with God's righteousness.

The natural family

Just as traditional marriages are decreasing as a proportion of all marriages, so too the traditional form of families is also decreasing. As time goes on, the increasing diversity in the form of marriages is developing into an increasing diversity in the form of families. In contemporary society, more children are likely to be with parents who are not married, than half of a century ago. More children are likely to have step-siblings and step-parents after parents have divorced and remarried. More children are likely to be with two adoptive parents of the same sex. Furthermore, some women are now choosing to have families on their own without a marriage partner. Women can now readily access advice on how they can become a single mother by choice.[3] Defining relationships as a family is not sufficient within itself to take on the righteousness of God.

Again, care and discernment are needed within the church. Secular influence could inadvertently result in the upholding of some family arrangements within the church that are not consistent with God's righteousness.

The family and persecution

Jesus made known to His followers that persecution would be experienced by those faithful to Him, telling them, 'if they persecute me, they will persecute you also' (John 15:20). Paul also explained, 'in fact, everyone who wants to live a godly life in Christ Jesus will be persecuted' (2 Timothy 3:12). Jesus made it quite clear that one place where this would be expected to occur would be within families (Matthew 10:21–22). Jesus told His followers that 'a man's enemies will be the members of his own household' (Matthew 10:36).

Situations arise in which strong opposition to Christ occurs within the family. Anyone in such a family who finds faith in Christ may bring division to the family. If guided by secular philosophy, those outside that family may want to deter or even prevent anyone within that family coming to faith in Christ due to the division it may cause. If 'family' is thought to be the most important element of building a society, then any disharmony within the family may be seen as detrimental to society. This secular view could lead to supporting harmony within a family, even if the harmony leads to spiritual darkness and eventually to spiritual destruction.

The word of God upholds honour, love and respect for others in the family (e.g., Exodus 20:12; Ephesians 5:22–25; Colossians 3:21; Ephesians 6:4; 1 Timothy 5:8) and love of

God within a family (Matthew 22:37; Deuteronomy 6:4–7). However, it also makes clear that even if society experiences a greater level of adoption of faith in Christ, division will still occur within families.

As goes the family, so goes the nation

One justification used by social policy makers to endorse a focus on, and elevation of, the family within society is based on social observation and research.[4] They argue that a correlation is found between the stability and health of families and the stability and health of a nation: in other words, when families are stable and healthy, so too is the nation. When the rate of breakdown of families increases, so too does the decline of the nation. At the *Family: Dare to Dream* conference in Melbourne in 2000, Pope John Paul II said, 'As the family goes … so goes society as a whole'.[5] A similar quote, 'as families go, so goes the nation,' is attributed to anthropologist Margaret Mead.[6]

Secular philosophers conclude that if we focus on building up families, concentrate our attention on supporting families and generally exalt the position of families within society, we will be building up our nation. However, within the church, we should look beyond human thoughts and wisdom and look to what we learn from God's wisdom.

If, as God's word tells us, it is Jesus, the Son of God, in whom all things hold together and who sustains all things by His powerful word (Colossians 1:17; Hebrews 1:3), then families, communities and nations are all built up by the same honour for God and by abiding by the same word of God. We need to carefully identify what is the cause and what is the effect. Is focusing on families the cause of a nation being strong, or is focusing on the powerful word of God the cause, with strong nations, communities, individuals and families being the effect?

The words of Pope John Paul II could easily be extended to relate to individuals and society: 'As the individual goes ... so goes society as a whole.' If individuals within a nation are balanced, stable, loving, peaceful and righteous, their nation will also be stable and righteous. If individuals within a nation are corrupt, a natural consequence is that the nation will also be corrupt. The word of God that sustains individuals is the same word of God that sustains nations. Jesus taught us to seek first God's kingdom and His righteousness (Matthew 6:33). This teaching is as relevant to individuals as it is to families or communities. God's word tells us that 'righteousness exalts a nation' (Proverbs 14:34), and it is reasonable to think that righteous individuals contribute to exalting a nation, as do righteous families and communities.

Members of our household

One significant statement made by Jesus in relation to the family seems, at first sight, to be quite radical; however, it warrants further reflection. What did Jesus mean when He said, 'If anyone comes to me and does not hate his own father and mother and wife and children and brothers and sisters, yes, and even his own life, he cannot be my disciple.' (Luke 14:26 ESV) Several observations can be made about this passage; however, comparing it first with a parallel passage helps to gain an understanding. Matthew recorded Jesus as saying:

> Anyone who loves their father or mother more than me is not worthy of me; anyone who loves their son or daughter more than me is not worthy of me. Whoever does not take their cross and follow me is not worthy of me. Whoever finds their life will lose it, and whoever loses their life for my sake will find it. (Matthew 10:37–39)

John Wesley, in his *Explanatory Notes of the Whole Bible,* explains that the use of 'hate' in Luke 14:26 is a comparative term.[7] The English language has limitations, and in describing how much greater our love for God ought to be than any other earthly affection, including that in our family relationships, we cannot easily describe anything greater than the difference between love and hate. Therefore, this difference is the most apt in describing how much greater our love of God should be than our love for our family, or for anything else. The explanation in *Gill's Exposition of the Whole Bible* is similar, explaining that although loving family relationships are envisaged in the Bible's teaching, nothing should be allowed to obstruct the honour or interests of Christ.[8]

Within any context, if anyone or anything is loved more than God, that affection falls within the ambit of idolatry. Therefore, Jesus' statement could be interpreted as saying that we should not allow our love for family to become idolatry but should keep that love within appropriate bounds.

Link between self and family

In Jesus' statement in Matthew 10:37–39, He is linking the attitude toward relationships within our family to the attitude we are to have for our own life, if we are to be His disciples. He firstly says that anyone who loves family members more than Him is not worthy of Him. Immediately afterwards, He says that whoever finds their life will lose it, and whoever loses their life for His sake will find it (Matthew 10:37–39). Jesus speaks of the two issues in the one statement and deals with them together. Shedding more light on how God wants us to view our own lives should, therefore, help our understanding of how He wants us to view these family relationships.

'Hating our own life' is mentioned in Luke 14:26. This appears to relate to what is commonly understood, that self-centredness and focusing on self-importance and self-interest would not only be ineffective in building up our own lives but would be detrimental and cause loss. Rejecting the temptation to place the self in a central position as we follow Jesus is likely to be what is inferred in Luke 14:26. 'Hating' our family relationships, as stated in this passage, similarly appears to advocate rejecting the temptation to place our natural family in a central position when functioning as the family of God. By considering Jesus' statement in this way, it is inappropriate for the church to take direction from and follow the secular view of a family-centred and family-focused approach to overcome the social pressures being experienced. To do so would be ineffective and would contribute to the social problems observed, rather than helping with the solution.

The measure of faith

Within our society, marriage and family relationships are generally the human relationships experienced most closely by people. Of all human relationships, they are the ones we hold most dearly in our hearts and where our greatest emotion and passion lie. It is against these relationships that our faith can best be measured and prioritised.

Abraham placed his belief in God immeasurably higher than his love for family. He was a man of faith (Galatians 3:9), and in believing God, this was credited to him as righteousness (Romans 4:3). In the example of Abraham, as with Jesus' statement in Luke 14:26 about family, faith is measured against our love for family. Faith is depicted as how absolute our love for God is, and therefore how far it is above our love for our most dear human relationships.

Looking to the future

The NCLS Report's[9] Table 3 shows the significant statistical decline of people affiliated with the Christian church in Australia, especially since the 1970s. As a strategy to address a similar decline, Wilson observes that some in the church in the British Isles view families as essential for church growth.[10] It is reasonable to think the same occurs in Australia. In some churches, almost all members are elderly, so the reasoning is that families and children are needed for these churches to survive for coming generations. This is used as justification for the church to focus on marriage and families and to prioritise catering for those who are married and those with families over those who are single and those without children. Rather than relying on God's word, this type of pragmatic approach depends on human wisdom and effort. However, God's word tells us that 'unless the LORD builds the house, the builders labour in vain' (Psalm 127:1). Unless Jesus builds His church (Matthew 16:18), our own contribution will ultimately be futile.

What is normal?

Another noticeable value judgement associated with favouring marriage and families within the church, is the one holding the view that marriage and families are considered 'normal' within the church and expected of most people.[11] However, it is questionable whether this is the most appropriate way of viewing the church community. Marriage and family are institutions of the natural world. In contrast, Jesus said that His kingdom is not of the natural world (John 18:36) and that His church consists of the people of the kingdom of God (see Matthew 13:38).

More appropriate ways could be used to describe what is normal for the people of His kingdom. Examples include: being born of the Spirit (John 3:5–6); being led by the Spirit (Romans 8:14); hearing the word of Jesus and putting it into practice (Matthew 7:24; Luke 8:21); being fruitful in the kingdom of God (John 15:16); and other similar matters of faith in which no distinction is made between those who are single and those who are married. The most appropriate expectations for what is normal within the church are found in becoming like the 'last Adam' rather than in the pattern of the 'first Adam'.[12]

Chapter 5

The Image of God

In building an understanding of the most appropriate way of approaching issues relating to marriage, families and singleness within the church, a single person's perspective is particularly relevant in two areas. The first relates to approaches influenced by secular philosophies that are inconsistent with God's word, resulting in singleness being portrayed unfavourably. The second relates to interpretations of God's word that favour marriages and families in ways that are not accurate representations of what God's word is really saying.

Previous chapters include discussion on approaches influenced by secular philosophies that are inconsistent with God's word and that have specific impacts on those who are single. This chapter begins a discussion on the interpretation of God's word in ways that are open to question and that affect the understanding of issues related to marriage, families and singleness.

In one of his Psalms, Israel's King David highlights the great value we can attribute to the word of God given to us in the Bible: 'The decrees of the LORD are firm, and all of them are righteous. They are more precious than gold, than much pure gold' (Psalm 19:9–10). Determining how God's word applies to any matter, and particularly to complex matters, can be likened to sifting through an array of ideas to discover the pure gold that lies among them. Considering the matters relating to marriage, family and singleness from a single person's perspective is beneficial in the sifting process. It ensures God's word is not unintentionally distorted by continually being interpreted from a family-focused point of view.

A significant concept

Marriage was instituted at the very beginning of creation, the narrative of which we find at the beginning of Genesis, the first book of the Bible. How we understand the positions of marriage, families and singleness in the church and society today can be greatly influenced by how we understand what God's word tells us about the event of creation. One very significant concept in God's word is that we are created in the image of God.

The meaning of the passage, 'So God created man in his own image, in the image of God he created him; male and female he created them' (Genesis 1:27 ESV), has great significance in understanding the position of marriage within the church. Is this passage in Genesis saying that the description, 'male and female', is included in the image of God? At first reading, this seems feasible. Or is the statement merely clarifying that those who are male, as well as those who are female, are made in the image of God, without attributing 'male and female' to the image of God? Although this may seem a small and insignificant distinction, it proves to be quite important.

How the 'image of God' is understood will influence how Genesis 1:27 is interpreted. This chapter discusses how our understanding of the image of God and this verse may shape our beliefs about marriage, family and singleness within the church.

The image of God

Widely diverse ideas are proposed for what is referred to by the phrase 'the image of God', but no direct statements in scripture define what it means, says Millard Erickson (2013) in his book, *Christian Theology*.[1] He then suggests that the image of God is only fully seen in a human being who is unspoiled by sin and the Fall.[2]

Attributes

Some attributes of God are described in scripture. The apostle Paul describes God as holy and righteous when he says '... put on the new self, created to be like God in true righteousness and holiness' (Ephesians 4:24). We read also that God is eternal (Psalm 90:2; Romans 16:26); God is light (1 John 1:5); God is love (1 John 4:8); and God is spirit (John 4:24). Jesus is the exact likeness of God (Hebrews 1:3) and He is truth (John 14:6; John 17:17). Other attributes that Erickson suggests may describe the image of God include being able to reason and recognise the truth[3], being able to exercise dominion[4] and experiencing a relationship.[5]

Without identifying any specific attributes, some general conclusions can be made about the image of God. The image, whatever it refers to, is unique to mankind among all of creation and distinguishes mankind from the animals. In creation, only mankind has been made in the image and likeness of God, says Erickson.[6] Also, whatever the image refers to, it enables us to relate to God. Jesus' relationship with the Father was characterised by fellowship, obedience and love, says Erickson.[7] As Jesus is the exact image of God (Hebrews 1:3), then developing the likeness of Christ within us (Romans 8:29) will develop the same characteristics of one created in that image, Erickson concludes.[8]

God's word describes Adam and Eve as created in God's image or likeness. When they have one of their children, Adam is described as having a son 'in his own likeness, in his own image, and he named him Seth' (Genesis 5:3). The explanation of some theologians is that Adam's son was born after sin had come into the world through Adam and Eve's disobedience to God, and thus Adam's son was born in his image, that is, as a sinner like Adam.[9]

Implications

The image also relates to our belonging to God. When questioned about paying tax to Caesar, Jesus asked the questioners whose image was on a coin. 'Caesar's', they replied. Then Jesus said to them, 'Render to Caesar the things that are Caesar's and to God the things that are God's' (Mark 12:13–17 ESV). The point made by Jesus is that, as the money of the realm displayed Caesar's image, it therefore belonged to Caesar, so it was right to give to Caesar what was his, says Erickson. Likewise, because we bear God's image, we belong to Him and therefore it is right to give ourselves to Him.[10]

We are made in God's image, says Erickson, so the image of God defines the essence of humanity for us.[11] Erickson reasons that the meaning we give to the image of God and the way that we understand the image will influence how we treat and minister to others. If our ability to reason is the attribute we associate with the image, then education and cognitive activities will be important in our dealings with others. If our ability to experience a relationship is how we understand the image, then, suggests Erickson, our ministry is more likely to focus on small group interaction, relationship-building activities and relational theology.[12]

Relevance today

To extrapolate Erickson's reasoning, if the image of God were to be viewed as including the description, 'male and female', this is likely to influence our understanding of the positions of marriage, families and singleness within the church. Whatever the meaning of the image, being created in the image of God is what makes us who we are, says Erickson.[13] By associating 'male and female' with the image of God and viewing humanity in that way, it seems likely that marriage, family and male–female relationships would become a significant focus within the church. They would be the outworking and expression of the image of God. Consequently, singleness would be likely to be seen in terms of non-fulfilment of the image that God intends us to express in our lives. If 'male and female' is not included in the attributes of the image of God, then marriage, family and male–female relationships would have much less emphasis. Whatever we understand as the image of God, the flow-on effect is likely to influence our whole ministry, our understanding of who we are and who we are meant to be and indeed, who God is and our whole theology.

Classifying the interpretations

Diverse ideas are proposed by theologians to explain the meaning of the phrase 'the image of God', with these ideas categorised into three broad groups by Erickson.[14] A brief overview of the different approaches enables a better understanding of how they influence the interpretation of Genesis 1:27 and shape our beliefs about marriage, family and singleness within the church.

The 'relational view' of the image of God incorporates those views based on an understanding of the image as being man's ability to relate to others and to God. The views based on what man is able to do are categorised by Erickson as a 'functional view'. Finally, a 'substantive view' is one that understands the image as consisting of characteristics within the nature of man that may be psychological, spiritual or physical.

A relational view

Karl Barth was one theologian who suggested that the image of God is relational, and that the image of God is the specific relationship that we have with Him and which we can have with other people.[15] We can relate to God and other people in a special way, just as God is able to relate to another, so we are, in a sense, a 'duplication' of the divine being.[16] Barth suggests that the image of God in which we are created is revealed within our relationships with one another, with specific reference to male–female relationships.[17] In reference to the creation of man in Genesis 1:27 and Genesis 5:1–2, Barth noted the coupling of the statements about man being created in God's image to statements about them being created male and female. He suggested that 'the image of God in man, then, is found in man's being created male and female'.[18]

The views held by Barth are among the less traditional views of the image of God, writes Erickson.[19] He concludes that Barth's arguments regarding the image of God being relational are flawed and not supported by sound reasoning.[20] Thus, it could be said that, although being created in the image of God enables man to relate to God and one's fellow man in a unique way that separates us from the animals, that relationship is not the image.

One facet of Barth's relational view of the image of God, that 'the image of God in man is found in man's being created male and female', is particularly relevant to the discussion on marriage, family and singleness within the church.

A functional view

In Genesis 1:27 and Genesis 5:1–2, the statement that God created man in his image is immediately followed by the statement that God created them male and female. This close association has led to the 'relational view' of the image of God as discussed above. A similarly close association occurs in Genesis 1:26 between the statement, 'Let us make

The Image of God

man in our image, in our likeness ...' and the statement, 'and let them have dominion ...'. The close connection here between these two statements, in God's expression of His intention to create man, is repeated in the following verses in the narrative of God's creation of man (Genesis 1:27–28 ESV). After God's creation of man, He immediately gives them the command to have dominion. This has led some theologians to suggest that the image of God in man is the dominion that man exercises over creation, that is, something which man does.[21]

Erickson evaluates this 'functional view' of the image of God as one providing another of the less traditional views of the image.[22] Erickson reasons, in part, that the word of God refers to man being created in God's image before man is given the command to have dominion and, therefore, man's dominion is not a sound concept of the image of God.[23] Man being created in God's image and man having dominion over creation are two distinct concepts. Being created in the image of God enables man to have dominion over creation. Erickson concludes that this, however, does not represent the image of God.[24]

One aspect of the 'functional view' of God's image is particularly relevant to our discussions on marriage, family and singleness within the church. In Genesis 1:28, the statement 'fill the earth' is connected to, and immediately followed by, the statement 'and subdue it'. Therefore, some theologians who hold the view that the image of God is seen in the man and woman in terms of their dominion or representative rule, also suggest that this representative rule is expressed in part by procreation.[25] This, therefore, infers that procreation is part of the expression of the image of God in the man and woman. If procreation is thus integral to the image of God in mankind, this would have enormous implications for the position of marriage and family in the church.

Referring to the earlier discussion about the image of God, Erickson suggests that the meaning of the image of God, as we understand it, will influence how we treat and minister to others and how we define humanity. Therefore, if, as suggested, procreation is an attribute of the image of God, it would have an impact on our understanding of the position of marriage, families and singleness within the church. This suggestion needs to be carefully evaluated.

The best evaluation of the image of God is to look at Jesus, because it is Jesus who reveals the Father to us (John 14:9) and He is the image of God (Colossians 1:15). If the image of God is seen in the man and woman in terms of their representative rule, and representative rule is expressed in part by procreation, then that is the image we should see when we look at Jesus. Clearly, we do not. Jesus is the exact likeness of God (Hebrews 1:3), but physical procreation was not part of His mission.

A substantive view

The final category provided by Erickson to explain the meaning of the image of God is the 'substantive view'.[26] This has been the dominant view through most of Christian history, with this view referring to an inherent characteristic or quality within a person's make-up.

One of the attributes theologians most commonly associate with the image of God is the ability to reason.[27] Erickson suggests that this may reflect their interest in a characteristic that is important to them.[28] To extrapolate Erickson's hypothesis, counsellors may say relationships are the most important attribute of the image of God, while musicians or artists would undoubtedly insist that creativity is the central attribute.

Interpretations of Genesis 1:27

Diverse ideas are proposed to explain the meaning of the phrase 'the image of God'. This leads to Genesis 1:27 being interpreted in a variety of ways. In relation to Genesis 1:27, two groups of interpretations warrant specific evaluation due to the significant impact they have on the understanding of marriage, families and singleness. The interpretations are: either 'male and female' included in the image of God; or 'male and female' not being included in the image of God.

Included in the image of God

If 'male and female' is included in the image of God, God would have all the male and all the female attributes, because the Bible says that there is only one true God (Deuteronomy 6:4). God is one: there are not two Gods, one male, the other female.

Interpretations that include 'male and female' in the image of God will have an impact on our understanding of Genesis 1:27. All the attributes unique to Adam when God created him could be defined as male attributes and all the attributes unique to Eve when God created her could be defined as female attributes. If 'male and female' is understood to be included in the image of God, Adam would have been created only partly in the image of God, being created a man. Likewise, Eve would have been created only partly in the image of God, being created a woman, even though they were both sinless when created.

If Genesis 1:27 is interpreted with 'male and female' included in the image, it would be a natural line of reasoning to conclude that when the first man and first woman were joined as husband and wife, they would have become more complete in the image of God than they were individually before the marriage. In the marriage relationship, they would have become 'one flesh' in God's sight (Genesis 2:24) with both male and female within that relationship. Therefore, together in that relationship they would have more fully exhibited the image of God. This interpretation introduces problems for how the position of marriage and singleness is viewed within the church.

The interpretation that includes 'male and female' in the image of God is also of concern in relation to gender identity. If we are created in the image of God, and 'male and female' is understood to be included in that image, then those who desire the prerogative to choose their own gender identity according to their own preference could find support in this interpretation.[29]

Not included in the image of God

In his article, 'The *imagio dei* as vocation'[30], Paul Sands comments on the differentiation of the two people God created as being male and female. He suggests that 'male and female' is an additional characteristic rather than relating to the preceding statement of being created in God's image. The phrase, 'male and female He created them' (Genesis 1:27 ESV) is a new idea, he says, that relates to the following verse on reproduction.[31]

Following on from Sand's interpretation, the use of singular and plural terms in Genesis 1:27 for the people created by God, may give a further clue to the meaning of the verse. The first part of the verse, 'so God created man in his own image' (Genesis 1:27a ESV), has the term 'man' in the singular. The second part, 'in the image of God he created him' (Genesis 1:27b ESV) uses, in the original text, the singular pronoun 'him'. By speaking in singular terms, it is reasonable to think that, within the context of 'the image of God', the first two people are the same and therefore spoken of together, both being made in the image of God.

In the third part of the verse, 'male and female he created them' (Genesis 1:27c ESV), the pronoun 'them' is plural. Here it is reasonable to think that, by using the plural pronoun 'them' within the context of gender, Adam and Eve are different and therefore are spoken of separately, with Adam being male and Eve being female.

The implication of this interpretation is that both Adam and Eve were created in the image of God, but that 'male and female' is not an attribute of the image of God. This implies, therefore, that marriage and singleness have no bearing on the completeness of the image. Thus, in the kingdom of God, those who are single have equal standing with those who are married.

The image of the invisible God

The observation by Erickson that no direct statements in scripture define the image of God[32] helps to explain why different people reach vastly different conclusions about what this term means. The objective of this chapter is not to reach a definitive resolution of what is meant by the image of God. Rather, three important outcomes relevant to our broader discussion on marriage, families and singleness are being pursued. The first is simply to acknowledge the diversity of interpretations. The second outcome is to recognise the large impact that each different interpretation of the image of God, and of Genesis 1:27, can have in understanding matters related to marriage, family and singleness. Thirdly, in the context of our discussion, understanding what 'the image of God' does not mean is a more profitable and obtainable outcome than attempting to understand what it does mean.

Diverse interpretations

Diverse ideas are proposed to explain the meaning of the phrase 'the image of God', hence, the various ways in which Genesis 1:27 is understood. Genesis 1:27, and the concept of the image of God, are both very important and should not be overlooked. However, the interpretation of this verse and concept needs to be carefully considered, as how they are understood can have enormous consequences.

Looking at these matters predominantly from either a marriage and family perspective or from a singleness perspective could lead to a distorted understanding of what God is saying. Any inaccurate interpretation could then affect nearly everything within the life of a church community. It could influence the position of marriage and families within the church and the value placed on them.

It could also greatly influence the way in which singleness is viewed.

In seeking to explore the issues surrounding marriage, family and singleness in any church situation, it is helpful to be aware of the prevailing theology of the image of God and the impact it can have on the understanding of the issues.

What the image of God does not mean

The following evaluation of the image of God is intended to ascertain what the image of God does not mean. It aims to question interpretations of the image that incorporate the description 'male and female' as an attribute included in the image of God. Such a description would imply a man and woman are more fully the image of God when they become married than they are as individuals before marriage. The evaluation also aims to question other interpretations of Genesis 1:27 which conclude that a man and woman are more fully the image of God when they become married than they are as individuals before marriage. The *Focus on the Family* web article titled, 'God and Man as Male and Female: Implications for Gender Identity', for example, suggests that, 'according to Genesis 1:27, it is only as these two distinct halves of humanity come together that the image of God in man is most fully and completely revealed'.[33] It seems that such a conclusion could only be reached if it was held that 'male and female' was an attribute included in the image of God. Yet the article maintains that 'male and female' is not an attribute of the image of God. However, the conclusion is what is being questioned, regardless of the reasoning behind the conclusion.

Our best understanding of the image of God is derived from our understanding of Jesus because He is the exact image of God (Colossians 1:15; Hebrews 1:3). Through this approach, problems emerge for interpretations that include 'male and female' in the image. We read in the word of God that Jesus 'is the image of the invisible God' (Colossians 1:15) and that He is 'the exact representation of His being' (Hebrews 1:3). However, scripture also says that for those 'in Christ Jesus', 'there is neither Jew nor Gentile, neither slave nor free, nor is there male and female' (Galatians 3:28). Why would the apostle Paul say there is not 'male and female' in Christ if this represents the very image of God in man? Paul's description that in Christ Jesus there is not 'male and female' appears to be synonymous with him saying that in the image of God there is not 'male and female'.

Looking further at Jesus, who is the image of God (Colossians 1:15), God tells us in His word that becoming transformed into that same image is His purpose for us (Romans 8:29). This transformation comes from the Spirit of the Lord, says Paul:

> Now the Lord is the Spirit, and where the Spirit of the Lord is, there is freedom. And we all, with unveiled face, beholding the glory of the Lord, are being transformed into the same image from one degree of glory to another. For this comes from the Lord who is the Spirit. (2 Corinthians 3:17–18 ESV)

Becoming more like Christ is the one way provided to us by God to become more fully the image of God. Jesus was not married, and becoming more like the first Adam through marriage is not a second way provided to us by God to become more fully the image of God. If this distinction is not made, it is easy to see how a misunderstanding of the position of marriage and singleness in the church could develop.

Chapter 6

An Overview of God's Plan

The Old Testament prophet Isaiah declared that God's ways and thoughts are higher than ours (Isaiah 55:9). As we explore God's word, we should then expect to find guidance and direction for dealing with the social problems facing the church and society from an insight beyond that upon which the world draws.

Clarification is needed on the correct biblical understanding of some situations, as was seen in the discussion in the previous chapter. To arrive at a sound biblical understanding, a good procedure, at times, is to go back to first principles, taking a 'ground-up' approach.

This chapter and Chapter 7 explore the scriptural basis for some of the biblical principles relating to marriage, family and singleness. These principles emerge from God's desire and plan to reconcile humanity to Himself. Throughout the history of God's relationship with His people, it is evident that God's plan of reconciliation was established before the creation of the world and will continue until the end of the world as we know it. The approach in this chapter and the following chapter is, firstly, to examine an overview of the narrative of God's relationship with His people, from both Old and New Testaments and, secondly, to suggest ways in which our biblical understanding of marriage, family and singleness stems from this narrative.

Overview — the Fall

In the biblical account of creation, at the end of the sixth day of creation, when God looked at all that He had made, He saw it was very good (Genesis 1:31). God placed the man and the woman in a pleasant and fruitful garden (Genesis 2:8–9; 2:22). They shared an unblemished relationship with Him until they rebelled against Him and He consequently banished them from the garden (Genesis 3:23). This is the first intrusion of sin into the world and owing to this 'fall' from what God intended the first man and woman to be, death came into God's previously very good creation (Romans 5:12). Adam and Eve could no longer reach their full potential as intended by God. This one act of disobedience led to the whole of creation becoming subject to frustration and decay (Romans 8:20–21). A sinful nature and death were passed on to all mankind (Romans 5:12;18–19). Mankind was powerless, on their own, to restore their relationship with God. They could not, through their own efforts, again become holy and righteous and so fulfil their purpose in creation.

To the serpent, who, by his lying and deception, had tempted the woman to disobey what God had said, God made a declaration: 'so the LORD God said to the serpent ... "I will put enmity between you and the woman, and between your offspring and hers; he will crush your head, and you will strike his heel"' (Genesis 3:14–15). At the very beginning, this was a revelation of God's plan and the promise of the 'Messiah' who would 'crush the head' of the serpent, and therefore make a way for humanity's relationship with God to be restored.

'The serpent' was originally a part of God's very good creation. He was a manifestation of Lucifer, one of God's highest angels who, through pride and rebellion, tried to make himself equal with God. He was therefore cast out of heaven (Isaiah 14:12–14) and is now called Satan or the devil. The power he has, until his head is crushed by the Messiah, comes through man's sin. Satan is the first and highest in the rebellion against God. Man's sin is also rebellion against God and His word and, as Jesus said, 'everyone who sins is a slave to sin' (John 8:34). God had given man dominion over the earth (Genesis 1:28; Psalm 115:16) but, at the fall of man into sin, man rebelled against God's design for us in creation and became a slave to sin. Satan therefore claimed dominion over the world through man's sin (1 John 5:19). He is now also referred to as the 'prince of this world' and will continue to be so, until his ultimate defeat by the Messiah, as God planned from the beginning.

God's promises to Abraham

At the very beginning, in the Garden of Eden, God said to the first man and woman, '… Be fruitful and increase in number …' (Genesis 1:28). Therefore, the human population of the world began to increase. God's word tells us that the unrighteousness of the population also increased and, at the time of Noah, 'all the people on the earth had corrupted their ways' (Genesis 6:12). However, Noah was a righteous man (Genesis 6:9). In judgement of the corruption and violence, God used a flood to destroy the world and its people (Genesis 6:13), with only Noah and seven others saved. Noah and his wife, his sons and their wives were all saved from the flood by entering the ark that God had instructed Noah to build.

The story of Noah provides an illustration of God's plan for how the 'offspring of the woman' would restore righteousness and man's unblemished relationship with God. As God destroyed violence and corruption at the time of Noah, so He will, in a time to come, again destroy all that is corrupt and unrighteous on the earth. However, this time it will be with fire (Hebrews 10:27; 2 Peter 3:7–12). It will be 'the offspring of the woman', God's chosen one, the Christ, who will, as did the ark, provide a way to escape the coming destruction. All who 'enter into' Christ will escape the destruction of the corruption and violence on the earth.

After the flood, the population of the earth again increased. God selected Abraham to be the father of His chosen people and God called him to leave the country in which he was living and to go to a place that God would show him. God made the promise, 'I will make you into a great nation, and I will bless you; I will make your name great, and you will be a blessing. I will bless those who bless you, and whoever curses you I will curse; and all people on earth will be blessed through you' (Genesis 12:2–3).

Abraham, at that time called Abram, was seventy-five years old and obeyed what God had asked of him. He and his wife were childless. His wife was old and beyond childbearing age (Genesis 18:11) but God promised him he would have a son and said to him, 'Look up at the sky and count the stars — if indeed you can count them ... so shall your offspring be' (Genesis 15:5). Abram believed God and this was credited to him as righteousness (Genesis 15:6).

At first, Abram and his wife relied on their own human understanding to try to bring about what God had promised. They reasoned that it would be impossible for Abram's wife to bear a child, so his wife gave him their Egyptian slave girl Hagar to bear his child. Subsequently,

Hagar gave birth to Ishmael. The consequence of Abram and his wife using human wisdom to try to bring about God's will would bring ongoing trouble (Genesis 16:12).

The Lord appeared to Abram and said, 'I am God Almighty; walk before me faithfully and be blameless. Then I will make my covenant between me and you and will greatly increase your numbers' (Genesis 17:1–2), renaming him Abraham (Genesis 17:5). God again promised Abraham that his wife Sarah would bear him a son and said, 'you will call him Isaac. I will establish my covenant with him as an everlasting covenant for his descendants after him' (Genesis 17:19). God said that He would surely bless Ishmael but 'my covenant I will establish with Isaac' (Genesis 17:21).

Abraham and his wife believed God and had a son as God had promised when Abraham was aged one hundred and his wife Sarah was about ninety. The apostle Paul later said, 'Against all hope, Abraham in hope believed and so became the father of many nations, just as it had been said to him, "so shall your offspring be"' (Romans 4:18).

God later tested Abraham. It was customary for Abraham to perform the religious practice of sacrificing animals (Genesis 15:9–10). However, on this occasion, God told him to take his son Isaac, the son born to Abraham in his old age, and sacrifice him on the mountain as a burnt offering (Genesis 22:1–2). God had promised Abraham that his offspring would be numbered as the stars in the sky (Genesis 15:5).

His son Isaac was the hope for God's promises to be fulfilled, but Abraham was then faced with God's request that he give up his son as a sacrifice. Believing and trusting in God, Abraham proceeded to do as requested. It was only when God saw that Abraham was truly prepared to go through with the request, that He stopped the sacrifice going ahead. Abraham had believed God and had placed his faith and hope in God at an immeasurably higher level than his hope in his natural family.

Abraham believed God and did not withhold his only son from Him; therefore, God again made a declaration that He would bless Abraham:

> I swear by myself, declares the Lord, that because you have done this and not withheld your son, your only son, I will surely bless you and make your descendants as numerous as the stars in the sky and the sand on the seashore. Your descendants will take possession of the cities of their enemies, and through your offspring all nations on earth will be blessed, because you have obeyed me. (Genesis 22:16–18)

Through the events of Abraham's life, God made more known about His plan to restore mankind. When God asked Abraham to sacrifice his son Isaac, even though God had said to him 'It is through Isaac that your offspring will be reckoned' (Hebrews 11:18), Abraham reasoned by faith that God could even raise the dead (Hebrews 11:19). This illustration foretold how God would sacrifice His own Son as the perfect sacrifice for the sin of mankind, and how this Son of God would rise from the dead to finally overcome death which had come into the world through sin.

Moses and the Passover

Jacob was the second born of Isaac's twin sons; however, the birthright and Isaac's blessing came to him. Jacob was renamed Israel by God and became the father of the twelve patriarchs of the nation of Israel (Acts 7:8). His descendants moved to live in Egypt and increased greatly in number. Eventually they became enslaved by the Egyptians until God sent Moses to lead them out of their bondage in Egypt.

On the night before they left Egypt, each Israelite household or group of neighbouring households killed a Passover lamb, and sprinkled blood on the sides and top of the doorframes of their houses as God had requested. This would protect them from the final plague God was to bring upon Egypt before they allowed the Israelites to leave. God had said, 'The blood will be a sign for you on the houses where you are, and when I see the blood, I will pass over you. No destructive plague will touch you when I strike Egypt' (Exodus 12:13).

This exodus of Israel from Egypt was also an illustration and foretelling of God's plan. As God's people were slaves in Egypt, so people become slaves to their sin. Jesus Himself said, 'Very truly I tell you, everyone who sins is a slave to sin' (John 8:34). God was foretelling how He would provide a perfect Passover lamb, the Messiah, whose blood would release those who came under its protection and would save them from the destruction that God would bring on the sin that held them captive.

After leading God's people out of their slavery in Egypt and crossing the Red Sea, Moses received, on Mount Sinai, two stone tablets of the Old Covenant Law which were inscribed by the finger of God (Exodus 31:18; Deuteronomy 9:10). The Old Covenant Law and the Prophets all pointed forward to the coming Messiah. Moses then led the Israelites to the threshold of the promised land, with this an illustration of how God's Messiah would lead God's people to the eternal promised land.

God's promise to David

After God's people entered the land that God promised them, it was King David who entered Jerusalem and established it as the nation's principal city. It was in Jerusalem that King David planned to build a 'house for God's Name' which would house the Ark of the Covenant. The Ark held the tablets of stone on which God had written the Law given to Moses (2 Samuel 7:2) after he led them out of Egypt. God promised David that he would 'never fail to have a successor on the throne of Israel' (1 Kings 9:5). However, God said to King David that it would not be him, but his successor who would 'build a house for my Name'.

It was King David's son Solomon, when he became king after David, who built the temple in Jerusalem. God spoke to Solomon and said:

> As for you, if you walk before me faithfully with integrity of heart and uprightness, as David your father did, and do all I command and observe my decrees and laws, I will establish your royal throne over Israel forever, as I promised David your father when I said, 'You shall never fail to have a successor on the throne of Israel'. (1 Kings 9:4–5)

This was God's word to Solomon; however, it was also a foretelling of the eternal kingdom of the promised Messiah.

Prophecy

Through the prophet Jeremiah, God made a promise like the one He had made to Abraham. He said, 'I will make the descendants of David my servant and the Levites who minister before me as countless as the stars in the sky and as measureless as the sand on the seashore' (Jeremiah 33:22).

The Old Testament prophets, by foretelling more of God's plan, added to what had been promised from the beginning. Jeremiah foretold that the coming Messiah would be a descendant of David, saying that:

> 'The days are coming', declares the Lord, 'when I will raise up for David a righteous Branch, a King who will reign

wisely and do what is just and right in the land. In his days Judah will be saved and Israel will live in safety. This is the name by which he will be called: The Lord Our Righteous Saviour'. (Jeremiah 23:5–6)

King David himself also foresaw the Messiah. The apostle Peter, when addressing the crowd on the day of Pentecost, described what King David had said about the Messiah:

I saw the Lord always before me. Because he is at my right hand, I will not be shaken. Therefore, my heart is glad and my tongue rejoices; my body also will rest in hope, because you will not abandon me to the realm of the dead, you will not let your holy one see decay. You have made known to me the paths of life; you will fill me with joy in your presence. (Acts 2:25–28)

Peter was quoting from Psalm 16. He continued by saying:

David died and was buried, and his tomb is in Jerusalem to this day. But he was a prophet and knew God had promised him on oath that he would place one of his descendants on his throne. Seeing what was to come, he spoke of the resurrection of the Messiah, that he was not abandoned to the realm of the dead, nor did his body see decay. (Acts 2:29–31)

The prophet Isaiah foretold more about the Messiah when he spoke of a 'suffering servant', saying:

> But He was pierced for our transgressions, He was crushed for our iniquities; the punishment that brought us peace was on him, and by his wounds we are healed. We all like sheep, have gone astray, each of us has turned to our own way; and the Lord has laid on him the iniquity of us all. (Isaiah 53:5–6)

The prophet Jeremiah foretold God's plan of making a new covenant with His people, saying: '"The days are coming," declares the LORD, "when I will make a new covenant with the people of Israel and with the people of Judah"' (Jeremiah 31:31) and '"I will put my law in their minds and write it on their hearts. I will be their God and they will be my people"' (Jeremiah 31:33).

Foretelling fulfilled

The fulfilment of what had been promised by God from the beginning was announced by the angel Gabriel to a virgin named Mary:

> Mary, you have found favour with God. You will conceive and give birth to a son, and you are to call him Jesus. He will be great and will be called the Son of the Most High. The Lord God will give him the throne of his father David, and he will reign over Jacob's descendants forever; his kingdom will never end. (Luke 1:31–33)

On hearing this, Mary gave her consent and answered, 'I am the servant of the Lord; let it be to me according to your word' (Luke 1:38 ESV).

Jesus was a biological descendant of King David and it was Jesus to whom God was referring when he said to King David that he would 'never fail to have a successor on the throne of Israel' (1Kings 9:5).

When Mary's child was born in Bethlehem, an angel of the Lord announced His birth to some shepherds keeping watch over their flock during the night: 'I bring you good news of great joy that will be for all the people. For unto you is born this day in the city of David, a saviour who is Christ the Lord. And this will be a sign to you: you will find a baby wrapped in swaddling cloths and lying in a manger' (Luke 2:10–12 ESV).

This child was the 'seed of the woman' who would overcome Satan, spoken of by God to Adam and Eve after sin first entered the world. This birth was of God's 'Promised One', the promised Messiah of whom God spoke through the prophets from the beginning. All of the Old Testament history and Covenant law pointed towards this birth.

When God chose Abraham, He made promises to him and to his seed. As the apostle Paul explains, 'The promises were spoken to Abraham and to his seed. Scripture does not say "and to seeds" meaning many people, but "and to your seed", meaning one person, who is Christ' (Galatians 3:16). The promises that God made to Abraham are therefore also made to us through Christ, as Paul again says, 'he redeemed us in order that the blessing given to Abraham might come to the Gentiles through Christ Jesus' (Galatians 3:14).

Abraham is seen as a great man of faith. God's word says, 'Abraham believed God, and it was credited to him as righteousness' (Galatians 3:6). He is not only understood to be the father of his own physical descendants, but also the father of those who by faith are now redeemed by Jesus Christ under the New Covenant, and who become the family of God. The apostle Paul says, '… those who have faith are children of Abraham' (Galatians 3:7).

The outcome of God's plan

In the book of Revelation, the end of this present earth and heaven and the coming of the new heaven and new earth are described. A description of the outcome of God's plan to restore mankind is also revealed. When all things are ready, God's restored people will be united with Jesus Christ in what is likened to a wedding celebration. That is the description of a future event, so before that time, God's people are preparing for what is ahead, like a bride making herself ready for her wedding. The present time is described in God's word as 'the last days', the final time period before the outcome of God's plan for humanity is realised (Hebrews 1:2; 1 Peter 1:20).

The first Adam and the last Adam

This overview of the biblical narrative of God's relationship with His people suggests a continuous plan from beginning to end. Viewing the issues we face today within the context of the whole of biblical history, contributes to the discussion that relates to marriage, families and singleness, in several ways. One of the ways is by contrasting the significance of the 'last Adam' to the 'first Adam'.

Adam was made from the dust of the earth (1 Corinthians 15:47; Genesis 2:7) but Jesus is from heaven (1 Corinthians 15:47; John 3:13,31). In contrasting Jesus with Adam, Paul describes Jesus as 'second Adam' or 'last Adam' and says, 'the first man Adam became a living being; the last Adam a life-giving spirit' (1 Corinthians 15:45).

Adam and Eve were the first married couple and, together with their children, formed the first family. Since then, marriages and families have followed the pattern they set. The secular approach of placing hope in marriage and families to build a community or nation places hope in the temporal pattern set by the first Adam.[1] However, the message given to the church is that the hope of humanity lies only with the spiritual pattern set by the 'last Adam'.

Hope of Israel

The Old Testament Jewish nation expected the arrival of a Messiah. At the time of Jesus, the general expectation of the nation was of a Messiah who would overthrow the occupying Romans and restore the physical kingdom of Israel.[2] Jesus' own disciples had imbibed the expectations of a temporal kingdom and on one occasion asked Him, 'Lord, are you at this time going to restore the kingdom to Israel?' (Acts 1:6).

However, Jesus revealed that the kingdom of God was not about the temporal world or outward observance. Jesus spoke of His kingdom saying, 'my kingdom is not of this world' (John 18:36) and 'the kingdom of God is within you' (Luke 17:21 KJV). This indicates God's plan to change the hearts of men rather than establishing a physical kingdom in the natural world. Jesus established the church as a spiritual family of faith rather than basing the church on natural family relationships.

Reflection

One question that emerges is how can the people of the kingdom of God, a kingdom 'not of this world', address the real and present problems of this world's cultural crisis, particularly the pressures exerted on marriage and families. This question is one of the key questions discussed in this book and one from which, in the broader Christian literature, a single person's perspective is often missing. This question is very relevant to single people because the way that the church addresses the question has significant implications for how single people are then treated in the church.

Jesus was sent into the world by His Father (John 17:18) and was anointed, as He said, 'to proclaim good news to the poor ... to proclaim freedom for the prisoners and recovery of sight for the blind, to set the oppressed free, to proclaim the year of the Lord's favour' (Luke 4:18–19). Likewise, Jesus sends His followers into the world (John 17:18; John 20:21). The outcome of the church seeking the kingdom of God (Matthew 6:33) is seen in the impact it has on the physical world, including issues related to marriage, families and singleness. Sin coming into the world brought physical death and decay (Romans 5:12; Rom 8:21). Forgiveness of sin through faith in Jesus Christ brings life, hope and restoration within marriages and families, and within singleness and our wider society.

Seeking first the kingdom of God and its righteousness (Matthew 6:33) and, consequently, exalting Jesus and heeding His words, foster values that we can uphold and which are beneficial to our temporal family relationships. Upholding the sanctity of marriage; upholding God-fearing relationships within a family; valuing parents bringing up their children in the training and instruction of the Lord (Ephesians 6:4; Deuteronomy 6:7; Proverbs 22:6); and children honouring their father and mother (Ephesians 6:1–2; Exodus 20:12) are all values which are fostered. God's word teaches us these values and, in the temporal world, marriage and families will find blessing and hope from upholding them. Those who are single also find life and hope in Jesus and in the example of His life because He too was single.

Chapter 7

The Beginning and the 'Last Days'

This chapter continues to explore the contribution to our discussion on marriage, family and singleness from considering the broad narrative of God's relationship with His people from beginning to end. The Old Testament nation of Israel was awaiting God's Messiah. The New Testament community of God's people live in the reality and victory of the resurrection of Jesus.

The place held by marriage, family and singleness within a community of faith is understood differently in each of the two testaments. God's word, as it relates to creation in the 'beginning,' continues to have important implications for our current understanding of marriage, families and singleness. However, care must be taken to determine what God is saying in a contemporary situation to avoid drawing misleading conclusions. This chapter examines some ideas that emerge and need careful evaluation.

Natural then spiritual

The apostle Paul points out that 'the spiritual did not come first, but the natural, and after that the spiritual' (1 Corinthians 15:46) and 'Just as we have borne the image of the earthly man, so shall we bear the image of the heavenly man' (1 Corinthians 15:49). While we now bear the perishable likeness of the first human being who was made from dust, we will bear the imperishable likeness of Christ in the resurrection.[1] Adam and all his offspring are from the dust of the earth and have inherited a sinful nature. All those who are 'in Christ' are born of the life-giving Spirit from heaven.

The last days

The coming of Jesus into the world was the central point of God's plan to reconcile man to Himself. It ushered in a time period referred to as the 'last days' (Hebrews 1:2; Acts 2:17). On the day of Pentecost, following Jesus' resurrection and ascension, the apostles gathered together in one place where they received the Spirit with power. The apostle Peter declared that this was in accordance with what the prophet Joel had said would happen in the last days. He indicated that the time to which the prophet Joel had referred to as the 'last days' was now upon them. The prophet Joel spoke of the 'last days' and said: 'In the last days, God says, I will pour out my Spirit on all people' (Acts 2:17). The apostle

Peter identified the happenings on the day of Pentecost as evidence of the coming of the 'last days'.

Following Pentecost, Peter continued referring to Jesus as having come in the 'last times' (1 Peter 1:20). The writer of the New Testament book of Hebrews also referred to the time in which he lived as being the 'last days', saying, 'In the past God spoke to our ancestors through the prophets at many times and in various ways, but in these last days he has spoken to us by his Son ...' (Hebrews 1:1–2).

Insight into our discussion on marriage, families and singleness can be gained by examining how God's word spoken in the 'beginning' now relates to our current time and circumstances, which are in the 'last days'.

A new birth

For the people in the 'beginning' who had originated from the dust of the ground, physical offspring were important to increase the population. God later said to Abraham, 'Look up at the sky and count the stars ... so shall your offspring be' (Genesis 15:5); thus, in the culture of the Old Testament nation of Israel, the bearing of physical descendants for Abraham was important. The expectation, also, was that, among Abraham's descendants, a Messiah would be born. Therefore, being barren meant not only failure to be part of fulfilling God's promise to Abraham of many descendants, but also being excluded from the hope of bearing the

Messiah. Bearing children was viewed as being included in God's plan for the salvation of His chosen people[2], with having children considered a blessing and evidence of God's favour. Therefore, barrenness was viewed as a 'reproach' or a 'disgrace', and was scorned.[3]

However, Jesus shed a new light on God's plan for salvation when he said we must be 'born again'. The apostle Peter said, 'For you have been born again, not of perishable seed, but of imperishable, through the living and enduring word of God' (1 Peter 1:23). Through the life Jesus lived and the words He spoke, He made it clear to us that it is faith that pleases God rather than physical descendants (Hebrews 11:6; Matthew 3:17; Matthew 17:20). The people of God, in the 'last days', are people born again of the Spirit and of imperishable seed, rather than a physical nation.

Just as we are born as babies into the physical world and grow to maturity, so it is with our eternal identity in Christ (John 3:6). To those young in faith, the apostle Peter says, 'Like newborn babies, crave pure spiritual milk, so that by it you may grow up in your salvation' (1 Peter 2:2). In speaking to those who should be more mature in faith, the writer of the New Testament book of Hebrews says:

> In fact, though by this time you ought to be teachers, you need someone to teach you the elementary truths of God's word all over again. You need milk, not solid food! Anyone who lives on milk, being still an infant, is not acquainted

with the teaching about righteousness. But solid food is for the mature, who by constant use have trained themselves to distinguish good from evil. (Hebrews 5:12–14)

A different perspective on family

Jesus introduced a different perspective on family relationships for the 'last days' to the cultural view held by the Old Testament nation of Israel. The people who Jesus primarily identified with as His family were those made holy through faith (Hebrews 2:11) rather than His natural family. The gospel of Luke describes an instance when Jesus' mother and brothers came to see Him but, due to the crowd, they were not able to get near Him. Someone told Him, 'Your mother and brothers are standing outside, wanting to see you'. He replied, 'My mother and my brothers are those who hear God's word and put it into practice' (Luke 8:20–21). Here, He was referring to the church. Although He respected His natural family relationships, He was saying He firstly regarded the church as His family.

For life in the 'last days', Jesus shifted His followers' cultural focus from the blessing of children in the natural world to the greater blessing of being in God's family. This is illustrated in the following situation that occurred when Jesus was speaking to a crowd of people. God's word describes the scene: 'As Jesus was saying these things, a woman in the crowd called out, "Blessed is the mother who gave you birth and nursed you'" (Luke 11:27). Jesus responded to her comment by saying, '"Blessed rather are those who hear the word of God and obey it"' (Luke 11:28). The description 'hear the word of God and obey it' reflects the manner in which Jesus redefined who He viewed as His family, when He said, 'My mother and my brothers are those who hear the word of God and do it' (Luke 8:21 ESV). Jesus refocuses our attention from the blessings of the natural world to the greater eternal blessings of the kingdom of God. He changes our focus from the blessing of having children, that the Old Testament nation of Israel understood, to the greater blessing of being made holy, hearing and obeying God's word, and becoming children in God's family in the 'last days'.

No longer alone

In the beginning, God said, 'It is not good for the man to be alone; I will make a helper suitable for him' (Genesis 2:18), so He created a woman as a helper for the man. Adam was made from the dust of the earth. God saw it was not good for the man to be alone so He created the woman and, subsequently, a family and community were formed. In the beginning, for Adam and Eve, marriage and family were an important aspect of being fruitful and increasing in number. In the 'last days', however, circumstances are different. When the first Adam was created, he was alone.

In the 'last days', we have an assurance that we will never be alone because Jesus is with us always (Matthew 28:20).

In the 'last days', Jesus is with the whole community of God's people, through His Spirit (Galatians 4:6), in a way not previously known (John 16:7; John 7:39; Acts 2:33; Galatians 3:14). It is only in the time after Jesus had ascended to heaven following His resurrection that the Spirit was sent with power to all who are in Christ. In the 'last days', Jesus is also with us through His 'body' which is the church. Jesus tells us that even in the very smallest gathering of the church, he is with us. He says, 'for where two or three gather in my name, there am I with them' (Matthew 18:20; also see Romans 8:9; 1 Corinthians 12:27; Ephesians 1:22–23). In the 'beginning', marriage, family and increasing the physical population were important for Adam and Eve. Jesus later refocused the attention of His followers. In the 'last days', the eternal and imperishable citizenship we have in God's family is the primary realm to which the people of God belong.

Helper

The word translated in Genesis 2:18 as 'helper' is the Hebrew word *'ezer* in the original text. In the Old Testament, the word *'ezer* is most frequently used to describe God as our helper. Examples are found in Deuteronomy 33:29, Psalm 27:9 and Hosea 13:9.[4] In Genesis 2:18, the concept of man not being alone is connected with the concept of there being a helper for him. These two concepts are also associated with each other in the New Testament with, again, reference to God being our helper. An example is found in the book of Hebrews: 'God has said, "Never will I leave you; never will I forsake you." So we say with confidence, "The Lord is my helper"' (Hebrews 13:5–6).

These two concepts are found together in the person of Jesus. He is an advocate on our behalf with the Father (1John 2:1; Hebrews 7:25; Hebrews 9:24) and He is with us always (Matthew 28:20). At the Last Supper, Jesus promised the Holy Spirit to His disciples saying, 'I will ask the Father, and He will give you another Helper, to be with you forever' (John 14:15–16 ESV). Thus, as with Jesus, the Holy Spirit is our advocate, or helper, and He does not leave us alone, but will be with us always.

In the beginning, God saw that Adam needed a helper so he would not be alone (Genesis 2:18). A different set of circumstances exist for those living in the 'last days'. Jesus is with us in a way that was not known in the 'beginning', so we are now no longer alone. Importantly, a part of experiencing His presence is through fellowship with His family of faith.

Alone does not mean single

The contemporary church's understanding of Genesis 2:18, 'It is not good for the man to be alone; I will make a helper suitable for him,' impacts on how issues relating to marriage, families and singleness are viewed.

What does it mean to not be alone? Does this mean that singleness is 'not good'? Is God saying that marriage and having a family is more pleasing to Him than singleness because marriage is 'good'? Did God's intention for Adam refer to him being married or to him belonging to the resultant community and therefore not being alone?

In the contemporary church in Australia, in my experience, it is not uncommon for the interpretation of Genesis 2:18 to be that, in God's view, it is 'not good' for a person to be single. Therefore, it is concluded that marriage and having a family is, in God's view, 'good' and more pleasing to Him than singleness. I would even suggest that, in the pews at a local church level, this interpretation of Genesis 2:18 is one of the most common theological reasons used for the undue elevation of the position of marriage within the contemporary church. However, this interpretation, and the conclusion that marriage and having a family is more pleasing to God than singleness, should be questioned. It does not give regard to Jesus' words that we are never alone because he is with us always if His Spirit dwells within us.

It also overlooks the apostle Paul's teaching when he advises some that it is good to not be married (1 Corinthians 7:8).

Fruitfulness

Jesus brought a more complete revelation of God's plan to the world. Through Him, a different perspective on a person being fruitful is revealed. In the beginning, God said to Adam and Eve, 'Be fruitful and increase in number' (Genesis 1:28). This same instruction was given earlier by God to the creatures of the water and the birds of the air after He had created them (Genesis 1:22). Therefore, this instruction appears to relate to the physical fruitfulness of having offspring and increasing the number of the physical population. The instruction God gave Adam and Eve to be fruitful and increase in number was an instruction God also later gave to Noah after the flood (Genesis 9:7) and to Jacob (Genesis 35:11). In the beginning, God called Adam to fill the earth with physical citizens. In contrast, in the 'last days', Jesus gave his disciples the great commission of making disciples of all nations, thus growing the citizenship of heaven.

No exemption

In relating the interpretation of Genesis 1:28 to the contemporary church, another question also emerges: are God's words to Adam and Eve a description of His instructions to them, or a prescription for them and for all following generations? Adam and Eve's offspring were all incorporated within the 'first Adam' at the 'beginning', says Robert Gundry (2010) in his *Commentary on the New Testament*.[5] Therefore, an interpretation that views God's words to Adam and Eve as God's command to them could be extended to imply that God's command was to all of Adam and Eve's descendants. *The Pulpit Commentary*, for example, interprets Genesis 2:18 as meaning that marriage, as a divine institution, is prescribed not only for the first pair but for all generations.[6]

If God's words to Adam are a command still applying to us today, this would have obvious implications for those who are single or childless. However, when an attempt is made to apply this interpretation to the contemporary church, inconsistencies emerge. The interpretation needs to be questioned, as it creates the idea that those who are married with families have obeyed the 'command' and therefore they are more righteous, in God's view, than those who are single and childless. This interpretation of Genesis 1:28 would support the view that marriage and having offspring are essential, or normal, within the Christian faith and within the church.[7] However, the authority of the life and example of Jesus Christ should lead to immediate dismissal of these ideas from our thinking. Jesus was completely obedient to His Father's will, and He did not consider it a command from God to marry and have physical offspring.

In an attempt to modify this view, some theologians propose the concept of the 'gift of singleness'. The reasoning used is that a select few have the 'gift of singleness' while, for the remainder of the contemporary church, marriage and families are either normal or expected.[8] The proposed concept of 'the gift of singleness' is primarily based on 1 Corinthians 7:7 and Matthew 19:11-12.[9] The concept of the 'gift of singleness' is described by some theologians as a *charisma,* or gift of the Spirit.[10] Chapter 9 discusses further this concept of the 'gift of singleness'.

The view that Genesis 1:28 is a command of God and still applicable to us today falls short when evaluated against the life of Jesus. This conclusion is not altered by the introduction of the concept of the 'gift of singleness'. A *charisma,* or gift of the Spirit, would not excuse or exempt a person from being obedient to one of God's commands. The prophet Ezekiel spoke the words given to him by God, saying, 'And I will put my Spirit in you and move you to follow my decrees and be careful to keep my laws' (Ezekiel 36:27). If God's words in Genesis 1:28 were a 'command' still applicable today, the command would also have applied to all past generations. The Holy Spirit would have strengthened and enabled all of God's people of past generations to abide by God's command. This would have included Jesus and the apostle Paul who were both unmarried, as well as all in the New Testament times who were not married.

The life and example of Jesus show that the words of Genesis 1:28 do not form a command that still applies to the contemporary church. Nor could the 'command' be applied selectively. Some hold the view that to 'be fruitful and increase in number' is God's command that today applies only to married couples.[11] However, this would create division whereas no division exists 'in Christ'. The family of God are one in Christ: the body of Christ is one body. Growing the citizenship of heaven is fruitfulness to which Jesus calls His church today.

The family of God is one body

This chapter earlier discussed the idea that marriage is more pleasing to God than singleness, based on Genesis 2:18 being interpreted as saying that singleness is 'not good' and that marriage is 'good'. Also discussed was the idea that marriage is more righteous in God's sight than singleness due to the belief that, today, marriage is still a command from God. In Chapter 5, an idea was discussed suggesting that marriage brings people more fully into the image of God. According to this idea, those who are married are more like God than those who are single.

When a higher and more privileged position is bestowed on marriage and families within society or the church due to these ideas, those who are childless or single or from broken marriages or broken families are devalued. However, God's way is that all in His family are one body who have equal concern for one another.

Jesus revealed that the kingdom of God was not about the temporal world or outward observance. He established the church as a spiritual family of faith rather than basing the church on natural family relationships. Two passages of scripture, Isaiah 56:3–5 and Galatians 4:22–27, use singleness to illustrate the greater freedom and life of God's eternal kingdom than what is found in the temporal world. They are discussed below.

A greater blessing

A contrast exists between the culture of the physical Jewish nation of Israel in the Old Testament and the more complete revelation of the kingdom of God in the New Testament. This chapter earlier discussed the cultural value placed by the Jewish nation on childbearing. In the Old Testament scripture, examples are found of passages describing the blessing of children. Psalm 127:3, for example, states that: 'Children are a heritage from the LORD, the fruit of the womb a reward.' Children were seen as the fulfilment of God's promise to Abraham of many descendants and, thus, barrenness was scorned. In the Old Testament culture of the nation of Israel, eunuchs were regarded as separated and degraded people.[12] However, God spoke through the prophet Isaiah telling how He would give to the eunuchs, who had no children, a blessing greater than childbearing. To the eunuchs who were faithful and righteous, God would give 'an everlasting name that will not be cut off' that is 'better than sons and daughters'.

> ... let no eunuch complain, 'I am only a dry tree'. For this is what the Lord says: 'To the eunuchs who keep my Sabbaths, who choose what pleases me and hold fast to my covenant — to them I will give within my temple and its walls a memorial and a name better than sons and daughters; I will give them an everlasting name that will endure forever. (Isaiah 56: 3–5)

Jesus, as the mediator of the New Covenant, brought a more complete illumination of God's plan and purpose. He shifted the cultural focus of the community of God's people from the blessing of children to the eternal blessing that was known, as seen in the above passage, but not fully realised. Under the New Covenant, those who are victorious through faith in Jesus Christ are viewed by God as holy and blameless in his sight. They are now called sons of God which is a new name given to them, says Gill.[13] This new name is an everlasting name that will not be cut off, a far greater heritage and blessing than sons and daughters.

Slavery and freedom

The apostle Paul uses a figurative illustration, or allegory, to establish a contrast between the slavery of the Old Covenant Law and believers in Jesus who are free from the Law, when he says:

> Abraham had two sons, one by the slave woman and the other by the free woman. His son by the slave woman was born according to the flesh, but his son by the free woman was born as the result of a divine promise. These things may be taken figuratively, for the women represent two covenants ... Now Hagar ... corresponds to the present city of Jerusalem, because she is in slavery with her children. But the Jerusalem that is above is free, and she is our mother. For it is written, 'Be glad, barren woman, you who never bore a child; shout for joy and cry aloud, you who were never in labour; because more are the children of the desolate woman than her who has a husband'. (Galatians 4:22–27)

The celebration, the freedom and the greater number of children is speaking figuratively of how the believers in Jesus receive an inheritance of eternal life and are free from slavery to the Law, says Gundry.[14] Paul is saying here that the barren and desolate woman should 'shout for joy and cry aloud' because of her freedom in Christ. The celebration for the one whose sins are forgiven in Christ is so much more than for the one who has sons and daughters. In speaking of release from slavery to sin, God's word says, 'if the Son sets you free, you will be free indeed' (John 8:36).

In relating this point to the discussion on marriage, families and singleness, the freedom in Christ is the same for those who are single or from broken marriages or broken families as it is for those who are married with children. It is from heaven that this restoration comes. It is not to the 'first Adam' or to marriage and families that society should look for restoration. It is only the 'last Adam' from heaven who can restore people within society and within marriages and families and in whom such hope can be found.

Chapter 8

Dealing with the Cause

As discussed in earlier chapters, the social change observed within our society over the past several decades is related to the movement away from, and increased rejection of, God's word in a general sense by our Western society. Understanding this as the cause then identifies the pressure on marriage and families as one of the symptoms of the direction chosen by our society.

This conclusion is consistent with the assessment made by Köstenberger and Jones when they suggest that the cultural crisis we are currently experiencing is a symptom of the spiritual crisis within our contemporary society.[1] The cause centres on the rejection of God's word, while the symptom is a cultural crisis. The pressure on marriages and families is one aspect of that cultural crisis.

The approach taken to address the pressure on marriages and families, in turn, has an impact on how singleness is viewed. In reflecting on matters relating to singleness within the church today, it is therefore necessary to be mindful of the preceding spiritual crisis within society. This crisis can be traced to the beginning of creation which is where this chapter starts the discussion. In going back to the beginning, the discussion considers the events in the Garden of Eden and the 'fall' of mankind from what God intended us to be. It then reflects on what it means when saying that a society is rejecting God and His word. The discussion moves on to examine the progression of the social change which we have experienced. The focus is on how the changing social conditions have been addressed in the past and how hindsight can help our understanding in dealing with issues today.

Trusting that God is good

Sin first entered the world in the Garden of Eden. In the account of creation in the book of Genesis, after God had created the man and woman, He gave them instructions, firstly, to be fruitful and fill the earth. Secondly, His instructions were to subdue the earth and to rule over it (Genesis 1:28). These instructions and this authority were given before Adam and Eve had sinned by disobeying God.

Although God gave the authority to rule to the man and woman before the 'Fall', now Satan is referred to as one who rules. He is called the 'prince of this world' (John 12:31), a position indicating rule over the world. Gill explains this by saying that Satan has usurped dominion. Benson indicates that Satan has obtained possession of dominion by sin and death.[2] Satan, then, has usurped the authority given to the man and woman through the effect of their sin.

The whole domain of *being fruitful and filling the earth* now comes under Satan's rule, for those not 'in Christ'. It is all a part of the fallen world. Evidence of this is found in the issues faced by our society and the church today. Gender identity, homosexuality, abortion, euthanasia, pornography, prostitution, sexual abuse and undermining of the parenting mandate are all among the issues that relate in some way to God's initial instruction to 'be fruitful and fill the earth'.

Selwyn Hughes suggests that the basis of the first sin in the Garden of Eden was not disobedience, but a failure to trust God.[3] Adam and Eve failed to trust that God had their best interests at heart when He forbade them to eat the fruit of the tree of the knowledge of good and evil. They then yielded to the temptation to follow their own desires rather than the righteous ways of God. Today, failure to trust that God has our best interests at heart has undoubtedly contributed to the social change.

Ministry of reconciliation

The problems faced within our society due to the social change are problems caused by sin. The authority that Satan has to rule in the area of procreation and its place within society comes only from our sin. Therefore, in overcoming the effects of sin, Satan's power is also overturned. This is what Jesus came to do (Hebrews 2:14; 1 John 3:8). The message of the cross of Christ is the only way to overcome Satan's rule. God's word tells us that the message of the cross is foolishness to those who are perishing (1 Corinthians 1:18) and to those who are enemies of God in their minds (Colossians 1:21; Romans 5:10). However, to those who are being saved, it is the power of God (1 Corinthians 1:18).

This explains why Paul says, 'Jews demand signs and Greeks seek wisdom, but we preach Christ crucified' (1 Corinthians 1:22–23), for it is 'preaching Christ crucified' that embodies the message of reconciliation with God which has been given to the church (2 Corinthians 5:18–19).

Delight in God's law

One of the most visible indications of the rejection of God in our society is the rejection of God's moral law. In our society, love as a virtue appears to be more an acceptable and positive attribute than upholding moral law. To many, love and the moral law are thought to be at opposite ends of a spectrum. However, although legalism and love may be at opposite ends of a spectrum, love and God's law are closely associated together in God's word (see John 15:10). The love referred to here is the love described by the Greek word *agape*. Matthew's gospel tells us of a time when Jesus was questioned about the law:

> Jesus replied: 'Love the Lord your God with all your heart and with all your soul and with all your mind.' This is the first and greatest commandment. And the second is like it: 'Love your neighbour as yourself.' All the Law and the Prophets hang on these two commandments. (Matthew 22:37–40)

Therefore, if a person was to fulfil God's law, they would be loving God and loving others with *agape* love. God's word also tells us how to know that we love: 'This is how we know that we love the children of God: by loving God and carrying out his commands. In fact, this is love for God: to keep his commands' (1 John 5:2–3). *Agape* love and the law point to the same attitudes and actions. *Agape* love and God's moral law both reflect God's nature and help us to understand who He is and the way He wants us to live.

To love God is not only to abide by God's law but to find delight in it. The psalmist says, 'Oh, how I love your law! I meditate on it all day long. Your commands are always with me and make me wiser than my enemies' (Psalm 119:97–98) and 'Great peace have those who love your law; and nothing can make them stumble' (Psalm 119:165). In the New Testament, the apostle Paul expresses the same sentiment, saying, 'For in my inner being I delight in God's law' (Romans 7:22).

Categories of biblical law

In briefly expanding on God's moral law and how it relates to the change in society in recent decades, it is worthwhile distinguishing between the different categories of biblical law. Some theologians divide biblical law into three main categories: civil law, ceremonial law and moral law.[4] The Old Covenant's civil law related to the people of the physical nation of Israel in the Old Testament and their relationship with God. As God's people are now a people of faith rather than a physical nation, the Old Covenant's civil law is no longer applicable to the church today. Ceremonial law pointed toward the Messiah, teaching us that 'without the shedding of blood there is no forgiveness' (Hebrews 9:22). These laws are fulfilled in Jesus, with his death being a perfect sacrifice made once for all. Therefore, the old ceremonial law is no longer applicable to us under the New Covenant. Moral law reflects God's nature and His will for us and shows us how to live in a way pleasing to Him. Although we are not justified by obedience to moral law, it remains relevant to us in understanding God's nature and His will.

Revealing sin

The apostle Paul spoke about the law, explaining that '... I would not have known what sin was had it not been for the law. For I would not have known what coveting really was if the law had not said "You shall not covet"' (Romans 7:7). He also said that, 'through the law we became conscious of our sin' (Romans 3:20).

From the beginning, God desired that we live in righteousness. However, after sin first came into the world, we had a distorted sense of righteousness. The prophet Isaiah spoke of this saying, 'All of us have become like one who is unclean, and all our righteous acts are like filthy rags' (Isaiah 64:6). We only know true righteousness when God reveals it to us. We only know the extent of our unrighteousness and sin through God revealing it to us, which happened through the giving of the law.

Our inability to fully observe God's law

During the times of the Old Testament, although God gave commands to His people for them to follow, they still could not walk with God in obedience as they had said they would (Exodus 19:8; Jeremiah 7:22–24). The apostle Paul observed something similar when writing to the Romans, saying that we are all 'under the power of sin' (Romans 3:9) from which we cannot free ourselves by our own efforts. He explained that the law would not bring about righteousness;

however, it would foreshadow and lead toward the one who God had promised from the beginning, through whom we might find righteousness and justification by faith (Galatians 3:19–24).

Although we become aware of our sin through the law, we are not able to free ourselves from the power of sin by obeying the law. This is the predicament of humanity that God planned to address from the very beginning. The sin that separates us from God, that we cannot deal with ourselves, has been dealt with by God who alone has the capacity to do so. This then summarises God's great plan for humanity from the beginning, to restore man's relationship with Him. Central to this plan is all that Jesus Christ achieved in coming into the world, dying and being raised again to life. As the apostle Peter writes:

> For you know that it was not with perishable things such as silver or gold that you were redeemed from the empty way of life handed down to you from your ancestors, but with the precious blood of Christ, a lamb without blemish or defect. He was chosen before the creation of the world, but was revealed in these last times for your sake. (1 Peter 1:18–20)

Following God's law

If those who desire to be obedient to God's law are not able to fully follow the requirements of God's law by their own efforts, then how much less able are those who do not have the desire to follow God's law? Those who are guided by the Spirit of God will delight in God's law (Psalm 119:18; 97–98; 165). However, over the past few decades, our society has increasingly been influenced not only by those who have no desire to follow God's law, but by those who delight in going against it.

A social trend

Within Australian society over the past fifty or sixty years, indications of a movement away from trusting God can be seen in the census data. In the 1960s, the majority of Australians identified themselves as being affiliated with Christianity. This included over 88% of the population, according to the national census data in both 1961 and 1966.[5] In the 1960s, less than 1% of the Australian population identified as having no religion. However, in the 2021 census, approximately 39% of the Australian population said they had no religious affiliation and 44% indicated an affiliation with Christianity.[6] An increasing number of people in our society are being guided by their own wisdom and desires, with a declining dependence on the guidance of the righteous ways of God. This correlates with the changes described by Daniel Yankelovich and Hugh Mackay that were observed around the 1970s. They described a social trend of 'looking after number one' and 'doing your own thing'.[7]

Progression

Before creation, God had already chosen us, in Christ, to be holy and blameless before Him (Ephesians 1:4). Blamelessness relates to doing no wrong. Holiness is concerned with being separate from the ordinary or the profane (see 2 Corinthians 6:12) and relates to being set apart for God.[8]

As a personal observation, a gradual shift is apparent in the way that the social change has expressed itself within Australian society over the past fifty or sixty years. The general movement away from trusting in God and His word has continued. However, in more recent decades, an increase in unholiness appears to have been added to unrighteousness within our society. It is no longer about simply choosing to do that which is contrary to God's righteous ways. A trend is occurring of choosing to define a person's identity by connection to that which is contrary to God's word and His created order. Due to this trend in society, the church increasingly needs to be attuned to God's call for holiness in addition to righteousness (see 1 Peter 1:16; 2 Corinthians 6:12).

A pressing concern

Philip Wilson draws attention to the importance for the church to determine the place of singleness and the family. He and American Christian ethicist Stanley Hauerwas both suggest that this is one of the most pressing concerns for the Western church today.[9] Other important issues may also exist, however, there is an acute need to address issues relating to singleness and families within the church.

A family-centric approach to addressing the effects of social change is not uncommon in Australia.[10] However, a single person's perspective, which could broaden the conversation and be of benefit in finding a solution, is often missing.

Prior to the change

In further reflecting on the social change of recent decades and how it has been addressed, this discussion will now examine some influences from the past and how they have shaped the social change. The starting point is to recall Philip Wilson's description of Victorian England. Wilson identifies the Victorian era novel as being influential in defining 'normality' within society. The image of normality created within many Victorian novels was of marriage being the desired destination and purpose in life.[11] The continuation of this influence into the twentieth century overlaps with a time during which Wilson suggests that Christianity was popular and important for most people; however, its prominence in their lives was declining.[12]

It is reasonable to think that a similar effect would be experienced in other Western cultures, including Australia. Early Hollywood films, prior to the middle of the twentieth century, also reinforced these same social norms.[13]

In Chapter 2, the Old Testament prophet Isaiah's words were recalled when he said that God's ways are higher than our ways (Isaiah 55:8–9). The discussion in Chapter 2 reflected on how God's righteous and true ways are higher than those of secular philosophy. The words of Isaiah are also just as true in relation to secular literature as they are to secular philosophy.

Godly marriage and families are good within themselves, as are romance and a love story. However, when secular literature paints a picture of marriage or families as the desired destination and purpose in life, it starts losing perspective. When our desire for something that has been created and has been given to us is greater than for the creator and giver of these good things, our desire is misplaced. This also applies when our ultimate purpose is found in what has been created rather than in the one who created it.

The language in God's word when Jesus tells His followers to 'seek first the kingdom of God' (Matthew 6:33 ESV) or when Paul instructs the Romans to 'offer your bodies as living sacrifices' (Romans 12:1) points toward God's kingdom being placed first. The temporal matters of life, although still important, are not our first priority.

The psalmist Asaph, for example, said, 'Whom have I in heaven but you? And earth has nothing I desire beside you' (Psalm 73:25). He and the apostle Paul (Philippians 3:8), both describe a desire for God greater than anything else on earth or in heaven. God has placed Jesus above all things in heaven and on earth and under the earth (Philippians 2:9–11). Our love for marriage and families, although still important, should not hinder or replace our love for God (Luke 14:26; Matthew 10:37).

The works of some Victorian novelists include a degree of Christian belief. However, if the overall moral of their story is that marriage is the desired destination and purpose in life, their writing is not constructing a biblical world view.

It appears to be a reasonable conclusion that, during the late nineteenth century and early twentieth century, a romantic view of marriage and families as the desired destination and purpose in life would have been fashionable due to the influence of literature and film. Western society's view of marriage and family at that time would have also been influenced by secular philosophy. It is likely that ideas stemming from philosophers like Aristotle and Erasmus, as discussed in Chapters 1 to 3, would have had influence across Western cultures, including Australia.

The change and the response

This background identifies one of the initial causes of the change to our social and moral norms experienced in the past 50 or 60 years. During the 1960s and 1970s something started happening that is still continuing today, and which has had an ongoing social and moral impact.

Both Wilson and Andrews identify social philosophies that have arisen since the 1960s that are aimed at deconstructing traditional marriage and families. These social philosophies are from the 'deconstruction' of marriage and the family end of the spectrum of secular ideas as discussed in Chapter 2. These philosophies are among the factors of that time that undermined the stability of both marriages and families. Following the 1960s, the rates of marriage and family breakdown began to increase.[14] Affiliation with the Christian church began to decline.[15] Today, a better understanding is still needed of what has happened and a solution still needs to be determined to address the ongoing impact of the ideas introduced by these philosophies.

Initiation of the problem

The dynamics of the social environment leading up to the 1960s and 1970s explain, at least in part, why these social philosophies, aiming for the deconstruction of the traditional family, arose at that time. By the middle of the twentieth century, marriage and having a family had become for many people the greatest desire, hope and purpose in life. Through the influence of secular philosophy, it is also likely that the family would have been viewed as necessary for people to flourish in life, as the foundation of society and as the institution that holds society together.

Within our fallen society, amongst us are those who, for their own spiritual and political agenda, seek to undermine the church and society. By the 1960s and 1970s, those who had such an agenda would have found marriage and the family, due to their exalted position, an irresistible target.

Impact on singleness

When marriage is believed to be our greatest destination and purpose in life, this inadvertently devalues singleness. It creates a belief that becoming married is the fulfilment of our destination and purpose. It implies that, unlike those who are married, those who are single, or from a broken marriage or broken family, are not fulfilled. However, God's word tells us that our ultimate fulfilment and purpose are found in Christ, not in marriage.

By faith, we know that, in Christ, we have been enriched in every way (1 Corinthians 1:5). In Christ, we have life to the full (John 10:10; Colossians 2:10) and we are always led in triumphal procession (2 Corinthians 2:14). This is the fulfilment that we have in Christ, whether we are married, single or from a broken marriage or broken family. The impact of the social change of the past few decades shows that marriages can be shaken. However, the kingdom we are receiving cannot be shaken (Hebrews 12:28).

By faith, we know that we were created in Christ for a purpose: 'to do the good works God has prepared in advance for us to do' (Ephesians 2:10). Whether we are married or single, that purpose is found only in Christ. It is not found in either marriage or in singleness. We have purpose due to the grace and salvation given to us in Christ (2 Timothy 1:9). God's word also tells us that, through faith in Christ, we are all equally a part of God's family (Galatians 3:26; Romans 12:5).

Shield of faith

The dynamics of the social environment during the 1960s and 1970s also explain why the forces aimed at the deconstruction of the family had such a significant impact. Although marriages and families are good and important within themselves, when they, rather than Christ, become our desired destination and purpose in life, they become a hindrance to our faith in God (Matthew 10:37-39).

The apostle Paul described faith as being like a shield when he said, 'Take up the shield of faith, with which you can extinguish all the flaming arrows of the evil one' (Ephesians 6:16). The parable of the wise and foolish builders, as told by Jesus (Matthew 7:24-27) and previously discussed, also points to faith in Him and His word being necessary for resilience against the forces aligned against us. Looking to marriage, rather than to Christ, as the desired destination and purpose in life is not a biblical posture of faith. It leaves marriages exposed and vulnerable to being undermined, lacking the shield of faith and the victory that it enables (1 John 5:4).

The contemporary situation

In the 1960s and the decades that followed, social philosophies aiming for the deconstruction of marriage and family became increasingly prominent. Relating this to Chapter 2's discussion, the 'deconstruction' philosophies are from one end of a spectrum of secular ideas on the value of marriage and families within society.

The response from those who opposed these 'deconstruction' philosophies was for marriage and families to be given a favoured and elevated position in both society and the church.[16] Ideas 'favouring' and exalting marriage and families are from the opposite end of the spectrum to social philosophies aiming for the 'deconstruction' of marriage and the family. In my experience, ideas from each end of the spectrum provoke and encourage a passionate response from people who hold views from the opposite end of the spectrum.

In the social environment of contemporary society, similarities are found to the social culture of a half-century ago. Although the forces aimed at the deconstruction of the family have changed in nature, they are still present. The cultural expression of marriage and family is changing and is different today to what it was in the 1960s and 1970s. However, for many, marriage is still the greatest desire, hope and purpose in life. Although the favouring of marriages and families and the exalting of their position and importance within society may occur in a different way today, it is still evident. Thus, a response is triggered today from those who want to undermine society and the church, as occurred in the 1960s and 1970s.

Self-perpetuating cycle

From my observation and experience over recent years, it appears that a pattern has developed in the way that social change is initiated and in how a response is drawn. Prior to the 1960s, the pattern was initiated when the position and status of marriage and families were raised through the influence of literature and film. Marriage and having a family became, for many people, the greatest desire, hope and purpose in life. This made marriage and families a target for the enemies of society and the church. It exposed them to being undermined without faith as a shield. Consequently, the rate of breakdown of marriages and families increased as the social change progressed.

The undermining of marriages and families elicited a response from those for whom marriage and having a family were the greatest desire, hope and purpose in life. Their response was to further raise the position and privilege of marriage and families within society. This, in turn, resulted in more undermining by provoking further response from the opposite end of the spectrum. More ways emerged to break down gender relations and identity, and to break down marriage relationships and family structure and relationships. This then drew a further response from those who favoured and privileged marriages and families, with an even greater focus on exalting their position. This made marriages and families an even larger target for those aiming to undermine the church and society. Thus, the process has continued in a self-perpetuating cycle.

Those who are single have become an unintended casualty of this cycle. The more the position and status of marriage and families are raised, the more singleness is devalued. However, another casualty of this cycle is marriage and families. This self-perpetuating cycle serves to trigger and foster their undermining. The church needs to guard against the influence of these secular responses to problems caused by sin.

Discussed earlier in this chapter was how social forces are under the rule of Satan owing to sin in the world. These social forces causing problems are not addressed by ideas from either end of the spectrum of secular ideas on the value of marriage and families within society. Only through the message of the cross of Christ and through faith are they overcome (1 Corinthians 1:18; 1 John 5:4). It is necessary to act in faith to carefully determine what God is saying. The suggestion of both Wilson and Hauerwas is that one of the most pressing concerns for the Western church is determining the place of singleness and the family. This idea certainly warrants further consideration.

Chapter 9

Being Single in God's Family

Is there a reason why single people are under-represented within the church? Are they, in fact, under-represented? Does this matter need to be addressed and, if so, how? The NCLS Report suggests that single people are under-represented in the church in Australia. The Report does not provide an explanation of why this occurs. It only presents data from a random sample once every five years, however, the data is from a nationwide sample, with the results providing a good reason to further explore the under-representation of single people within the church.

To do justice to any inquiry into the lack of single people within the church, the conversation needs to include the topic of marriage and family. Our dealings with singleness within the church are intricately connected to dealings with marriage and family, with a flow-on effect from one sphere to the other. This explains why the previous chapters have focused to such an extent on matters related to marriage and family, and why Chapter 10 returns to drawing conclusions on these matters. However, this chapter's focus is commenting on various issues related more specifically to singleness and the church.

Is being single a gift?

We know from God's word that it is Christ who holds all things together and sustains all things by His powerful word (Colossians 1:17; Hebrews 1:3). Care needs to be taken, however, when we seek to understand what 'his powerful word' is saying, that we hear what He is saying and not a meaning implied from our own partiality. Some confusion and misunderstanding surround the idea of the 'gift of singleness', a term that often appears in Christian literature and conversation. This idea warrants closer examination and clarification.

Examples are found in the New Testament of single people, both young and old, who were involved in the early Christian church's life and ministry. Single people include Jesus, John the Baptist, the apostle Paul, Anna the prophetess and the four daughters of Philip the evangelist. Others also, such as Mary, Martha and Lazarus from Bethany and Lydia from Thyatira were possibly unmarried. It does not seem likely, then, that marriage and family were an expectation within the early church. The apostle Paul even specifically taught that it was better not to be married (1 Corinthians 7:27–38).

These examples should end speculation that marriage and families are expected as normal, or even considered by some as essential, for those within the contemporary church. However, uncertainty continues to exist and is prolonged by the concept of the 'gift of singleness'. The reasoning used is that a select few have the 'gift of singleness' while, for the remainder of the contemporary church, marriage and families are either normal or expected.[1]

The proposition put forward by some, that singleness is a gift from God, is primarily based on 1 Corinthians 7:7 and Matthew 19:11–12.[2] In 1 Corinthians 7:7, the apostle Paul says, 'For I would that all men were even as I myself am. However, each man has his own gift from God, one in this manner and another in that' (KJV 2000). As Paul was single, some interpret this passage to mean that he was referring to 'being single' as a gift from God.[3] However, many earlier Bible commentators consider that this passage is saying something quite different. Ellicott's *Commentary for English Readers* specifically makes the comment that the apostle Paul is not saying that everyone should be unmarried as he is: rather, he is referring to continence (i.e., self-control) as the gift with which he was endowed.[4] Likewise, in *Barnes' Notes on the Bible*, it is suggested that the apostle Paul would be glad for everyone to have control of their passions, as he had, and that the gift to which he referred was the gift of continence.[5] In a similar way, *Matthew Poole's Commentary*, *Gill's Exposition of the Entire*

Bible and the *Pulpit Commentary* all suggest that the gift to which he referred is the gift of continency.[6] *Meyer's New Testament Commentary* also suggests that the apostle Paul is speaking of restraint, and that the gift is that of continency.[7]

Matthew 19:11–12 follows Jesus' response to a question from some Pharisees about divorce. Jesus' disciples commented on the words He had spoken to the Pharisees and made the statement, 'If such is the case of a man and his wife, it is better not to marry' (Matthew 19:10 ESV). Jesus responded to His disciples, saying to them:

> Not everyone can receive this saying, but only to whom it is given. For there are eunuchs who have been so from birth, and there are eunuchs who have been made eunuchs by men, and there are eunuchs who have made themselves eunuchs for the sake of the kingdom of heaven. Let the one who is able to receive this receive it. (Matthew 19:11–12 ESV)

Jesus' statements, 'Not everyone can receive this saying, but only to whom it is given' and 'there are eunuchs who have made themselves eunuchs for the sake of the kingdom of heaven,' are used to support the idea that Paul was referring to singleness as a gift in 1 Corinthians 7:7.[8]

When God gives

If singleness were a gift from God, it seems reasonable to think it would be either a gift of a physical nature or of a spiritual nature. Both these options should be included in a closer examination. Firstly, is it a gift of a physical nature?

Adam and Eve were created single, and everyone is born single. In terms of a physical designation, being single is how we all are, unless something occurs to change the way we all begin life. God can lead us to a godly spouse (Proverbs 19:14). However, apart from marriage, being single is how we remain. Until we are married, we do not need to be given singleness because that is how we all are by default.

To say that singleness is a physical gift from God, then, appears to be saying that God would give us a gift of … nothing! Without the 'gift', we are still single, if indeed that is the way we are. If we were given the physical 'gift' of singleness, nothing would change. For those who are married, to receive the 'gift' of singleness would mean the loss of a spouse, through death or divorce. It seems quite inappropriate to refer to the loss of a spouse as a 'gift' from God. Divorce is not God's plan for anyone (Mark 10:9; Romans 7:2) and death is spoken of as an enemy (1 Corinthians 15:26).

It is evident that God is more able and inclined to give good gifts to His children than people are to their own children

(Matthew 7:9–11). It is difficult to imagine that any parent would take an empty cardboard box, wrap it in elegant paper, tie a colourful ribbon around it and then present it to their child as a gift. How much more difficult is it, then, to imagine God giving a gift of nothing to one of His own precious children? It does not seem feasible to think of singleness as a gift of a physical nature from God. However, could it be a spiritual gift?

Not a spiritual gift

Examining Matthew 19:11–12 and 1 Corinthians 7:7 together suggests that singleness is not the gift referred to by either Jesus or Paul. In Matthew 19:11–12, Jesus says, 'not everyone can receive this saying, but only to whom it is given'. Jesus is stating that 'this saying' is what is being given. 'This saying' could either be referring to the rule Jesus laid down relating to divorce (Matthew 19:8–9) or to the disciples' comment that, 'it is better not to marry' (Matthew 19:10), says Ellicott.[9] He then says that the context indicates that 'this saying' is referring to the disciples' comment that 'it is better not to marry' (Matthew 19:10).

Following this, Jesus spoke about three groups of people who were unmarried. The principles underlying His response regarding these unmarried eunuchs appear to be principles that can be applied to those who are single in the contemporary church.

Jesus spoke of one group who were voluntarily eunuchs for the sake of the kingdom of heaven. Their condition was something they chose for themselves; thus, it was not a spiritual gift given by God. Even if someone were to ask God today for a spiritual gift, it is something given by God through His sovereign choice rather than being self-acquired or chosen by the individual. In the second group, some were born that way. Singleness is not a gift given only to some at birth. As discussed above, we are all born single. Finally, in the case of the third group of eunuchs, the condition was chosen for them by other people, not by God. It appears, then, in this passage, that Jesus was not describing singleness as a spiritual gift given by God. Jesus was describing how the statement made by His disciples, 'it is better not to marry,' could not be received by everyone, but only by those to whom it is given. Following on from His example of the unmarried eunuchs, Jesus then said, 'Let the one who is able to receive this receive it' (Matthew 19:12 ESV). Singleness, then, is not the gift but, rather, the gift is the ability to be single, which is an important distinction.

In the apostle Paul's comments recorded in 1 Corinthians 7:8–9, he speaks more broadly about those people who are able to receive the saying 'it is better not to marry'. He speaks of one's need to be married or one's capacity not to be married in terms of continence, or self-control. Paul says, 'To the unmarried and the widows I say that it is good for them to remain single, as I am. But if they cannot exercise self-control, they should marry. For it is better to marry than to burn with passion' (1 Corinthians 7:8–9 ESV). Therefore, there is good reason to believe that self-control is the gift to which Paul refers rather than singleness. Paul Barnett, in his commentary *1 Corinthians — Holiness and hope of a rescued people*, says, 'One's need to be married or one's capacity not to be is called a *charisma*.'[10] The 'capacity not to be' of which he speaks is in line with the 'continence' of earlier commentaries.

In pondering whether singleness is a spiritual gift, the nature of singleness should also be considered. Jesus described the nature of His kingdom by saying, 'My kingdom is not of this world' (John 18:36). Marriage and family are institutions of the temporal, natural world, while singleness is a term used to describe a person who is not part of the institution of marriage. The status of singleness belongs to the natural world and is apart from the realm of God's eternal kingdom, which is spiritual in nature. Therefore, it does not seem feasible for singleness to be referred to as a spiritual gift.

Evaluating the interpretations

It is not uncommon for more recent Bible commentators and theologians to support the concept of the gift of singleness.[11] Köstenberger and Jones, Danylak and Prior, for example, speak of the 'gift of singleness' as a *charisma*, or gift of the Spirit.[12] Danylak provides the following definition for 'the *charisma* of singleness':

> The *charisma* of singleness is a Spirit-enabled freedom to serve the King and the kingdom wholeheartedly, without undue distraction for the longings of sexual intimacy, marriage, and family.[13]

He continues, clarifying his definition, by saying, 'The gift of singleness is not simply the situation or status of being unmarried ...: it is divine enablement with a specific purpose.'[14] Marriage, however, is a temporal institution (Matthew 22:30). Therefore, the status of being unmarried is a temporal status and should be dismissed from being a part of a spiritual gift. The divine enablement to which Danylak refers, describes a spiritual gift with which a single person may be endowed; however, identification of the gift needs further consideration.

Freedom is described as one aspect of singleness in Danylak's definition. The apostle Paul speaks of freedom in the context of marriage and singleness, saying, 'I would like you to be free from concern. An unmarried man is concerned about the Lord's affairs — how he can please the Lord. But a married man is concerned about the affairs of the world — how he can please his wife' (1 Corinthians 7:32–33). The freedom of which Paul is speaking is not a freedom that is received from singleness being given as a gift. Everyone begins life with this freedom. The difference comes through those who are married choosing to surrender this freedom. This freedom has a practical and physical aspect, that is, freedom from married life's day-to-day concerns.

A much more internal aspect of freedom needs to be considered, namely, freedom of the heart to serve God wholeheartedly and with purpose. However, the freedom to serve God wholeheartedly and with purpose can also be found in people who are married. Thus, although the gift being described may be found in single people, singleness is not the gift.

One of the gifts of the Spirit is the gift of faith (1 Corinthians 12:9). Abraham was described as a man of faith. The biblical narrative of Abraham's life suggests that he had a sound and loving relationship with his family. He also had the freedom to serve God wholeheartedly, without his love for his family being a distraction. He demonstrated this in his willingness to sacrifice his son Isaac.[15] In the contemporary church, a married person who finds their fulfilment in Christ and not in family, could, like Abraham, have the freedom to serve God wholeheartedly without being distracted by their love for their family, or by the fulfilling of their physical desires. Faith is also spoken of by Jesus. He taught that faith is required to enable His followers to achieve the purposes of His kingdom (Matthew 17:20).

Self-control and faith are both spiritual qualities: it is feasible that both can be, and are, given by God as a gift to those in His family. However, singleness is a temporal characteristic. The reference made by contemporary theologians and commentators to the 'gift of singleness' is more in keeping with the description of either the gift of continence (or self-control) to which the apostle Paul referred or to the spiritual gift of faith in a single person. Clarifying this helps to avoid any misunderstanding, because, in my experience, confusion often arises when reference is made to 'the gift of singleness'. At a local church level, this is most often taken to mean that the physical status of singleness is a gift from God.

God's word highlights an advantage of being unmarried for the person who belongs to God's family, in that they may have greater opportunity to serve God (1 Corinthians 7:32–35) and to use their spiritual gifts. These gifts could be gifts of prophecy, preaching, teaching, serving, leading, showing mercy or one of many other gifts (Ephesians 4:11–13; 1 Corinthians 12:7–11; Romams 12:6–8). However, the spiritual gifts are the God-given abilities that serve Him and His purpose, rather than singleness per se. Singleness may allow greater scope for the gifts to be used but singleness is not the gift.

Thus, if singleness is not a spiritual gift, how then can the position of singleness be understood in the context of the community of God's people? What we know is that God guides all people who belong to His family (Ephesians 2:10). He may guide a single person in their life in such a way that they remain single. God may call someone to a life of singleness and He may empower someone to live life as a single person. He may take any situation in which we find ourselves, including being single, and achieve His great purpose through the gifts He gives. However, singleness is simply a description of a person who is not married rather than something that can be given as a gift. The suggestion that God's word describes singleness, itself, as a gift, is questionable and without a sound basis.

The concept of the 'gift of singleness' has, at times, been used in conjunction with the idea of marriage and families being normal and expected within the church.[16] However, this creates a temporal, organisational division within the church between those who are married and those who are single. Being a part of God's family and being faithful to Him is what should be normal and expected within the church.

The world's misleading wisdom

The wisdom and importance of hearing and following Jesus' words, rather than following human 'wisdom', cannot be overstated. The psalmist says, 'Your word is a lamp to my feet and a light to my path' (Psalm 119:105 ESV). Jesus' words guide us along a path that leads to life, even if that path is narrow and difficult (Matthew 7:14). The broad and easy path on which the wisdom of the world takes us, leads to destruction (Matthew 7:13).

How worldly wisdom can be misleading for single people amidst the anxiety and emotions of the desire to become married, experienced deeply by some, is worthy of reflection. Consider the saying, 'It's better to have loved and lost than never to have loved at all.' It is commonly used, easily remembered, catchy and, when used in its original context, is meritorious. However, when applied out of its original context, it can be used to convey worldly wisdom within our social culture that is quite misleading to those who are single. It is an extract from the literature of more than a century and a half ago, popularised in today's culture through social media, TV, film and popular music.[17]

The saying comes from the 1850 poem *In Memoriam A. H. H.* by Alfred Lord Tennyson in which he writes of the deep pain and grief felt at the death of a close friend.[18] Tennyson was trying to come to terms with the pain of his loss. He reasoned to himself that it would only have been if he had not even come to know his friend at all, that he could have escaped the pain he was feeling at the time of loss. He reasoned, then, that the joy in knowing his friend was greater than the grief he felt in the loss of that friend. So he wrote the words, ''Tis better to have loved and lost than never to have loved at all.'

However, when this saying is taken from its original context of bereavement and applied instead to romantic love in the context of marriage, it becomes misleading, both to single people within the church and to those outside. When applied to marriage, the saying appears to encourage those approaching marriage to consider that, even if their marriage were to fail, it would be better for them to have been married than to have remained single and never married at all.

Elements in marriage that are not in common with bereavement are that, in marriage, it is God who joins the two together, with marriage solemnised by vows. Jesus says about marriage, 'What therefore God has joined together, let not man separate' (Mark 10:9 ESV). Regarding the marriage vows, for example, ''till death do we part', God's word says, 'It is better not to make a vow than to make one and not fulfil it' (Ecclesiastes 5:5). Therefore, the saying, 'it's better to have loved and lost than never to have loved at all,' when applied to the context of marriage rather than to the context of bereavement, is contrary to the wisdom we find in God's word.

The wisdom of God's word regarding marriage finds some support in social psychology studies. Social psychologist and author, Bella DePaulo, commented on this matter in her article, 'is it better to have loved and lost than never to have loved at all?'[19] She refers to psychology studies and says that, based on survey data, if love is defined in terms of marriage, the answer to the question is 'no'. In almost every area studied, including happiness, health and longevity, results are more favourable for those who have always been single than for those who have been married and no longer are, either through divorce or the loss of a spouse.

Looking further

One of the most evident consequences of the cultural change over the past fifty or so years has been the increased rate of the breakdown of marriages in our society. The saying, 'It's better to have loved and lost than never to have loved at all,' when applied to marriage, reinforces the acceptance of the idea that marriage is no longer a lifelong bond in the way that it was created to be by God.

It is not unrealistic to think that wherever Tennyson's poetic line is popularised, it would become a part of 'social wisdom' of that community. It may create a view that it is simply 'common knowledge' that a failed marriage is better for a person than remaining single.

The problem of this mindset can be accentuated for single people when the status of marriage is raised and becomes a central focus within their community. This community mindset may lead to unfavourable attitudes toward those who are single, and create unnecessary anxiety about not being married. A single person may feel social pressure to become married.

When the idea that it's better to have loved and lost, is found together with social pressure to become married, in the same social environment, it creates a treacherous cocktail of ideas for those who are single. These ideas could lead to more lightly entering into marriage. They could create an unhealthier outlook. The ultimate end of the marriage would be less unexpected than it otherwise may have been.

Building our faith and lives well by hearing and acting on the guidance provided by Jesus' words becomes important in this situation. This can best be done within a social environment and mindset in which a person's acceptance and security lie in the position they have in Christ rather than in their marriage.

God chooses us

God has had a plan for humanity from before the beginning of creation. The working out of that plan will continue beyond the end of the world that we currently know. By hearing and putting into practice Jesus' words, we are connected to this plan, as God desires.

One important aspect of our involvement in God's plan can be found in the passage in which Jesus says, 'You did not choose me, but I chose you and appointed you to go and bear fruit — fruit that will last' (John 15:16). When we choose something, whatever it may be, we decide between two or more alternatives; otherwise, it would not be a choice. We evaluate, or judge, the alternatives against the purpose we have in mind for the choice we make. If it was us who chose God, this would involve our evaluation or judgement of God and His purpose for us. We would need to evaluate how our belief in Him could contribute to the purpose that we have decided to follow in our lives. However, we do not choose God, because it is God who chooses us to fulfil His purpose. Before the creation of the world, God chose that He would act to reconcile us to Himself and make us holy and blameless in His sight (Ephesians 1:4; Colossians 1:21–22) so we could be fruitful in the individual purpose He has tailored for each of us in our lives (John 15:16; Proverbs 19:21; Philippians 2:12–13).

The wedding banquet

This is illustrated in Jesus' parable about the wedding banquet (Matthew 22:1–14; Luke 14:16–24). In this parable, Jesus explains what the kingdom of God is like (Matthew 22:2):

> A certain man was preparing a great banquet and invited many guests. At the time of the banquet he sent His servants to tell those who had been invited, 'Come, for everything is now ready'. But they all alike began to make excuses ...'I have just bought a field' ...'I have just bought oxen' ...'I just

> got married' ... 'please excuse me ... I cannot come' (Luke 14:16-20). Then he said to his servants, 'The ... banquet is ready, but those I invited did not deserve to come. So go to the street corners and invite to the banquet anyone you find.' (Matthew 22:8–9)

This parable appears to be largely about the Jewish nation, that as a whole, did not receive the Messiah. Thus the gospel was subsequently taken to the Gentiles. However, it still illustrates the principle involved, that we do not choose God but He chooses us. In terms of the parable, the meaning would be that we do not invite ourselves to His banquet. It is God who chooses to invite us.

Reconciliation with God, then, is not an intellectual response to a set of beliefs held by another person or church that we choose to follow. Rather it is a personal heart response to the God who created us and who, by His love for us, chooses and invites us to be reconciled to Him. God also draws us to Himself and enables us to respond to His invitation (John 6:44, John 6:65).

The parable goes on to say, 'But when the king came in to see the guests, he noticed a man there who was not wearing wedding clothes ... the king told the attendants, "Tie him hand and foot, and throw him outside, into the darkness"' (Matthew 22:11–13). The parable suggests here that there are two decisions to be made by anyone wanting to share in the wedding banquet. The first is the decision whether to accept the invitation to the banquet, and the second is the decision whether to be clothed in appropriate wedding attire. Most of the wedding guests naturally made the two decisions together as one. They attended the wedding dressed in appropriate wedding attire. However, the king noticed one guest who did not.

In ancient times, in Eastern countries, it was customary for guests at royal banquets and weddings to be provided with festive garments to wear. To not wear the garments provided would be considered an insult to the host.[20] To what then in the parable is the symbolic wedding attire referring? Possible meanings come from other scriptural references. In a reference to the symbolic final wedding of Christ and the Church described in the book of Revelation, the bright and clean wedding garments represent the righteous acts of God's holy people (Revelation 19:7–8). In his prophecy of the Messiah, the Old Testament prophet Isaiah also described symbolic garments, saying, 'He has clothed me with garments of salvation and arrayed me in a robe of his righteousness' (Isaiah 61:10).

In commentary on the wedding garments mentioned in this parable (Matthew 22:11–13), Ellicott and Benson suggest that they refer to holiness, while Matthew Henry, Robert Jamieson, A.R. Fausset and David Brown, Barnes and Gill all allude to the wedding garments being related to putting on the righteousness of Christ.[21]

One way of viewing the parable is in the context of God's plan from the beginning of creation to the end of the world as we know it. It is then reasonable to conclude that the wedding attire for the banquet after the end of time relates to the purpose God expressed for us before the beginning. Before the creation of the world, God chose that we be holy and blameless in His sight (Ephesians 1:4). Therefore, it would be appropriate for those wanting to participate in the final wedding banquet to have been made holy and righteous as God desires.

Although commentators interpret the meaning of the parable in different ways, it is evident that God provides the garments for us to wear. Whichever way the parable is interpreted, the overall message is the same. The hope of welcomed participation in the final wedding banquet is by being made holy and righteous through repentance and faith in Christ.

God chooses the lowly

In this parable of the kingdom of God, and in God choosing us, no reason appears for why single people should be under-represented among His people. God does not want anyone to perish (2 Peter 3:9), but for all to come to repentance (2 Peter 3:9; 1 Timothy 2:4), including single people. God has a greater interest in the faith of the people who seek Him than in their temporal interests and institutions.

One might even expect single people to be over-represented within the church. God's word tells us that 'God chose the lowly things of this world and the despised things — and the things that are not — to nullify the things that are' (1 Corinthians 1:28). When Jesus was born into the world, the social culture of the time afforded marriage and families a high position, while those who were single held a lowly position. Similarly, in contemporary society, secular philosophers assign preferential standing to marriage and families. Single people are assigned a more inconsequential position. Therefore, if any group were to be over-represented, it seems that God might choose more single people in His kingdom. This is not because they are single, but because they are more likely to hold a position that our society considers to be of less worth. God could then use them, as He said, to nullify the things that the world exalts in a way that God does not.

People of faith

This chapter earlier discussed a passage that makes reference to fruitfulness saying, 'You did not choose me, but I chose you, and appointed you so you should go and bear fruit, and that your fruit should remain' (John 15:16 NKJV). In speaking to His followers, Jesus also makes reference to fruitfulness saying, 'I am the vine; you are the branches. He who abides in me and I in him, bears much fruit; for without me you can do nothing' (John 15:5 NKJV). Only when we receive Christ and remain in Him, like a branch grafted onto a vine, can we build our faith and lives well. Both these passages refer to eternal fruitfulness as an integral part of living in the kingdom of God.

Reconciliation with God; the holiness and righteousness that God has chosen for us; building our faith and life on a solid foundation; and fruitfulness for the kingdom of God, all revolve around a life of faith in Jesus Christ. They all seem to be equally available and applicable to single people as they are to anyone else. Those within the church are chosen to be a people of faith (Hebrews 12:2) and people of the kingdom of God (Matthew 13:38). In looking at a life of faith from this perspective, no apparent reason can be found for why single people should be under-represented in the church.

Seeing things differently

In relation to hearing Jesus' words and putting them into practice, we are not able to do this based solely on our own strength and understanding. To receive Christ and remain in Him, and to hear and do what He says, we are dependent on the guidance of the Holy Spirit. It is the Holy Spirit who guides us into all truth (John 16:13) and reminds us of everything that Jesus has said (John 14:26). We read in God's word:

> For the Spirit searches all things, yes, the deep things of God. For what man knows the things of a man except the spirit of the man which is in him? Even so no one knows the things of God except the Spirit of God ... But the natural man does not receive the things of the Spirit of God, for they are foolishness to him, nor can he know them, because they are spiritually discerned. (1 Corinthians 2:10–14 NKJV)

Another important matter to consider therefore, when hearing and doing what Jesus says, is that the world will see things differently.

A century ago, even fifty years ago, according to Australia's national census, most people growing up in Australia listed themselves as affiliated with the Christian church.[22] Therefore, it would be likely they would have had opportunity to hear the stories of the Bible. Increasingly now, however, the same does not occur. Those who follow the ways of the world live differently than those who honour God and follow His ways. An increased level of difference is developing between these two groups.

The psalmist's experience

In the context of a similar social environment in which contrasting views are apparent, the writer of Psalm 73 expresses feelings that any Christian today may also experience, but that can become particularly relevant for those who are single. This psalm is attributed to Asaph, one of David's Levitical choir leaders.[23] It begins by saying:

> Surely God is good ... to those who are pure in heart. But as for me, my feet had almost slipped; I had nearly lost my foothold. For I envied the arrogant when I saw the prosperity of the wicked. (Psalm 73:1–3)

Here the psalmist knows that God is good to the pure in heart but he experiences a crisis in faith when seeing the apparent prosperity of those who have rejected God and His ways. He continues:

> They have no struggles; their bodies are healthy and strong. They are free from the common human burdens; they are not plagued by human ills ... from their callous hearts comes iniquity; their evil imaginations have no limits ... they say, 'How would God know? Does the Most High know anything?' This is what the wicked are like — always carefree, they go on amassing wealth. (Psalm 73: 4–12)

The psalmist observes that everything seems to go well for the wicked, even though they delight in disregarding God. They do this in a way that seems to defy God and question whether He even knows what they do. After observing this, the psalmist questions whether maintaining his own faith is in vain, and reveals his struggle to deal with this matter. He continues:

> Surely in vain have I kept my heart pure and have I washed my hands in innocence. All day long I have been

afflicted; and every morning brings new punishments ... when I tried to understand all this, it troubled me deeply. (Psalm 73:13–16)

Beyond this point in the psalm, however, it becomes apparent that the psalmist has overcome his doubt and disillusionment and regained a strong and vibrant faith and that he is looking back to what is now past. He is acknowledging a critical time of uncertainty when he had great doubts, then recalls:

> ... 'till I entered the sanctuary of God; then I understood their final destiny. Surely you place them on slippery ground; you cast them down to ruin. How suddenly are they destroyed, completely swept away by terrors! (Psalm 73:17–19)

When he enters the sanctuary of God, he acquires a different outlook. He sees things from an eternal perspective. He then looks back at how he was before:

> When my heart was grieved and my spirit embittered, I was senseless and ignorant; I was a brute beast before You. Yet I am always with you; you hold me by my right hand. You guide me with your counsel, and afterward you will take me into glory ... my flesh and my heart may fail, but God is the strength of my heart and my portion forever ... (Psalm 73:21–25)

This passage highlights and commends the value of entering the sanctuary of God for the Old Testament psalmist. The

Old Testament people of Israel would draw close to God and come into His presence in the sanctuary. The sanctuary would be found in the tabernacle or temple of God. In these 'last days' of the New Testament times, God has sent His Spirit to be with us always (John 14:16; John 15:26). We can now draw near to God anywhere, not only in a specific place like the sanctuary.

We can draw near to God when we gather together with others in His family. Jesus said, 'For where two or three gather in my name, there am I with them' (Matthew 18:20). For Christians today, gathering together in Jesus' name and worshipping God are important practices. In the New Testament book of Hebrews, we read, 'let us … not give up meeting together, as some are in the habit of doing, but encouraging one another — and all the more as you see the Day approaching' (Hebrews 10:25).

Today, the word 'sanctuary' refers to the room in a church or chapel consecrated to the worship of God, or one in which worship services are held. Therefore, it is still common today to draw near to God in the sanctuary. However, it is because we are meeting with the people of God's family rather than because of the place itself, as in the Old Testament. The meeting together of those who are reconciled with God is an important aspect of Jesus' teaching. Jesus refers to us as His 'family' (Matthew 12:50; Luke 8:21) and His 'body' (1 Corinthians 12:27; Colossians 1:18).

In light of the NCLS Report and the under-representation of single people in the church that it shows, Psalm 73 and Hebrews 10:25 are of significance to single people. These passages serve as an encouragement to us to not become separated from the body of the church. An inherent significance is also found within this passage for the church as a whole. It is an encouragement to ensure that those who are single are welcomed and incorporated into the life of the church community in the same way as all others who are likewise reconciled with God in holiness and righteousness.

Although secular philosophy focuses on the centrality of our natural family, Jesus tells us that His followers will be distinguished by the *agape* love they have for the family of God. This includes those who are single in the same way as it does all others.

Tough love

In the New Testament, more light is shed on the type of challenge faced by the writer of Psalm 73 when he envied the wicked. This is worthwhile to reflect upon briefly. The psalmist observed the wicked being free of burdens, carefree and prosperous, thus questioning the value of his own faith in keeping his heart pure and washing his own hands in innocence (Psalm 73:1–16). He was suffering hardship while the wicked were not, so he questioned the benefit of continuing to live in righteousness.

The writer of the New Testament book of Hebrews changes the angle from which we view this situation by saying that enduring hardship is of invaluable benefit to us. The writer says,

> The Lord disciplines the one he loves, and chastens everyone he accepts as his son. Endure hardship as discipline; God is treating you as His children ... God disciplines us for our good, in order that we may share in His holiness. (Hebrews 12:6–10)

Our perspective is altered even further by the very sobering statements made by the apostle Paul to the Romans. He speaks of those who are so determined to constantly follow their own sinful desires and reject God's ways that God gives them over to their depravity and the inevitable destruction that follows. Three times in succession, Paul speaks of how a time comes when God gives people over to the desires they are adamantly following:

> Therefore God gave them over in the sinful desires of their hearts ... God gave them over to shameful lusts ... furthermore, just as they did not think it worthwhile to retain the knowledge of God, so God gave them over to a depraved mind, so that they do what ought not to be done. (Romans 1: 24–28)

Later in the same letter to the Romans, Paul tells how he rejoices in his own suffering. Although it is not wise to look for unnecessary suffering, we can be so thankful that God is able to use the hardships and suffering that come our way to discipline us so that 'we may share in His holiness' (Hebrews 12:10). How very thankful we can be when God shows us His tough love and does not give us over to our sinful desires but treats us as His children.

Chapter 10

Closing Reflections

Much of the discussion of previous chapters has aimed to advance the conversation relating to marriage, families and singleness by exploring the situation from a single person's perspective. The aim of this final chapter is to bring together the threads of discussion from previous chapters. Although the immediate discussion will be brought to a conclusion, the topic will be left open to further expansion as much more could be said.

The dilemma

No favouritism exists with God; however, numerous ideas discussed in previous chapters endorse preferential treatment for marriage and families within the church. This may inadvertently lead to a dilemma. What then is the position of single people? This dilemma appears to be more common than would be desired.

It is important to consider the dilemma of 'where do single people fit in the church?' However, the question is not always framed in this way. At times, it is more along the lines of 'do single people fit within the church?' Some view the church as 'a family of families',[1] while some regard marriage and families as an essential part of Christian faith.[2] In line with these schools of thought, do single people even fit within the church at all? Digging deeply to get to the bottom of this matter is what is needed if it is to be addressed in a way that is both effective and lasting.

Oblivious

In considering how best to support single people within the church community, one thing has become evident to me during my lifetime as a single person. Those who are married and have not experienced singleness to a great degree in their adult life can be quite oblivious to the flow-on impact on single people of the way that marriage and families are viewed and treated within the church. An approach taken to address the pressures on marriage and families can be entirely sincere, with no intention of devaluing singleness, but the negative impacts on those who are single can, even though inadvertent, still be significant.

God's word is 'a lamp to my feet and a light to my path' (Psalm 119:105 ESV), guiding us in the right way to build up all of God's family. Within the context of guidance for God's people as a community, intuitively, my feeling has been that a single person's perspective can provide important insight. The unique consequences of a single person's experience can help to unveil, and shed light on, the blind spot of many approaches to dealing with marriage and families that unintentionally impact on those who are single.

This input could potentially be beneficial to a church regardless of whether single people are impacted by that church's approach to marriage and families. Just as a driver driving a car along a multi-lane highway, with a blind spot behind and to one side, is assisted by a blind-spot mirror, so it is with a single person's perspective. If the blind-spot mirror reveals no hazard in the blind spot, the driver can manoeuvre into another lane with confidence. If a hazard exists, the blind-spot mirror aids the driver in making a decision to avoid any potential trouble.

A church may take an approach to matters relating to marriage and families that is not detrimental to single people. Making the blind spot visible, and showing the absence of any detrimental impacts upon single people, can still be of assistance. The church can have greater confidence in its chosen approach. If a church is approaching matters relating to marriage and families in a way that negatively impacts on those who are single, that church can also benefit. By seeing the blind spot and becoming aware of the detrimental impacts on single people, that church will be enabled to choose an approach that is more empathetic to single people.

Ambient acceptance

Reflecting on the passage of scripture, 'There should be no division in the body, but ... its parts should have equal concern for each other ... you are the body of Christ, and each one of you is a part of it' (1 Corinthians 12:25–27), reveals a biblical approach to singleness that is different to the world's approach. The discussion in previous chapters included reflection on how some secular philosophies advocate for preferential treatment and favouritism to be given to marriage and families. This is in response to the social change and the pressures faced by marriages and families within modern society. However, this can lead to a low and negative view of singleness. In contrast, in God's kingdom, His purpose is for everyone to have equal concern for each other and for everyone to be equally a part of the spiritual family of God. The biblical approach and the world's approach have a significantly different impact on single people.

Because the world and the church are guided by such different principles, single people might be expected to gravitate to the church where they would find acceptance, value and purpose beyond what is found in the world. This is not to say that the church should focus on those who are single, just as it should not focus on those who are married or who have families. The church is called by God to focus on seeking first His kingdom and its righteousness and to set our minds 'on things above, not on earthly things' (Colossians 3:2). However, in doing this, the ambient acceptance experienced within the church community by those who are single might be anticipated to be more widespread and wholehearted than they would experience in the wider society. This supports Wilson's suggestion that the church could be one of the best places for a single person to be.[3]

New challenges

The Bible, which is God's inspired word to us, is authentic in presenting an account of the lives of people of faith. It is not orchestrated or sanitised to present only a clean-cut version of the way people have lived and acted. It does not only describe how people have succeeded, been faithful and always done what is righteous. It equally describes people's weaknesses and failures. These include Jonah heading by sea for Tarshish instead of overland to Nineveh where God had sent him; Sarah giving her slave girl Hagar to Abraham, taking matters into their own hands to try to achieve God's purpose; and the apostle Peter denying Jesus three times. The weaknesses and failures of people are presented in a 'warts-and-all' account of their lives. A significant feature of the way that God deals with His people is that those who are weak and have failed have still become great people of faith through God's love and grace toward them.

For the first Christians, applying faith to their experiences in life was testing at times. The apostle Paul, for example, rebuked the apostle Peter over how he was confusing circumcision and the Old Covenant law with justification through faith in Jesus alone (Galatians 2:11–21). Paul was saying that you cannot take some of the requirements of the Old Covenant and mix them with some of the requirements of the New Covenant (Galatians 5:3).

The social change experienced in our society over the past several decades has precipitated our own challenges today. Should marriage and families again become a central element of the culture of the people of God? Should marriage and families again become the foundational institution on which the church and society are built?

A superficial similarity can be found between the position given to marriage and the family by social researchers from our contemporary secular society and the position given to marriage and the family within the Old Covenant community. The Old Covenant community incorporated marriage and having children within the central focus of their culture. Therefore, it is not a foreign concept in the Old Testament biblical literature that marriage and having children be given an elevated position within society.

However, Jesus took a different approach. When Jesus began His ministry on earth, as the mediator of the New Covenant, he established God's family as a family of faith rather than a physical family or physical nation. The family of faith was established as the central institution within the culture of the New Covenant community.

The message of Scripture is that it is only through a New Covenant approach, with the church acting as one body and with Jesus as the Head, that the instability in our contemporary society will be addressed.

Looking forward

Marriage acts as a signpost pointing to what is to come. Our earthly marriages point forward, toward a more perfect spiritual marriage at the end of time between Christ and the church (Ephesians 5:32; Revelation 19:7). Although our earthly marriages now are imperfect, the spiritual marriage between Christ and the church will be perfect. In the 'age to come', imperfect physical marriage will be no more (Luke 20:35).

This expresses our expectation of 'the age to come'. However, some aspects of the future spiritual marriage between Christ and the church are a part of our relationship with Christ now, before that time. The apostle Paul says, 'he anointed us, set his seal of ownership on us, and put his Spirit in our hearts as a deposit, guaranteeing what is to come' (2 Corinthians

1:22). The perfect has not yet fully come to us, although it has in part through the indwelling of the Holy Spirit.

Paul also looks forward through faith and says, 'For we know in part ... but when the perfect comes, the partial will pass away' (1 Corinthians 13:10 ESV). When Jesus came as mediator of the New Covenant, He shifted our focus away from our earthly families as the central institution of the people of God toward the eternal family of faith. The family of God are now those who have been born of the Spirit of God with a guarantee of what is to come.

The direction in which God's word takes us is reflected in the apostle Paul's approach of looking forward, not back: 'I press on to take hold of that for which Christ Jesus took hold of me ... forgetting what is behind and straining toward what is ahead' (Philippians 3:12–13). For us today, the Old Covenant approach of giving a central focus to marriage and procreation would be looking backward. The culture of the Old Covenant community was centred on physical childbearing as an inheritance of God's promises. Barrenness and singleness were held in low esteem. However, this approach does not present a way for us today of looking forward and taking hold of that for which Christ Jesus has taken hold of us.

Marriage and families are important and will continue to be a part of our temporal identities and our natural communities in this world until Christ returns (Matthew

24:37–39; Luke 17:26–30). The biblical expectation of *agape* love within our marriage and family relationships remains as high as it has always been. However, they are not the primary purpose for which Jesus has called us. Under the New Covenant, it is those born of the Spirit of God, with faith in Jesus, the Messiah, who are the family of God. Neither being married nor being single has any bearing on whether we, like Paul, are able to take hold of that for which Christ Jesus has taken hold of us.

God's guidance

Wilson observed that marriage is not a major topic of conversation in the New Testament writings.[4] In the apostle Paul's reference to marriage, he says that it is good not to be married (1 Corinthians 7:8). We read in God's word that His desire for us is that we become more like his Son, Jesus (2 Corinthians 3:18; Romans 8:29). This is not saying that His desire is for us all to be single like Jesus (1 Timothy 4:3). By extension, it is also not saying that He wants us all to become married, because Jesus was single. Whether we are married or single is only secondary to what God desires for us. Jesus was holy and righteous and God's desire is that we become more like Him in moral character.[5]

Jesus equally cares for and supports those who are single as He does those who are married or who have families. We are not alone for He is always with us and will be until the end of the age (Matthew 28:20). He is with us through His Spirit (John 14:16; Galatians 4:6) and through His body, the church, even in its smallest representation of two or three people (Matthew 18:20). This describes the community of faith that Jesus came to establish.

Final word

The NCLS Report identifies the under-representation of single people within the contemporary church community in Australia. The trend in the National Census statistics shows that over the past fifty or so years, single people have become an increasing proportion of the Australian population.[6] Therefore, understanding the position of single people within the church in Australia is becoming a growing concern.

Although the statistics do not answer the question of why this is occurring, they provide a good reason to further explore the matter to find out what is occurring and why. A conversation is needed within the church to determine why single people are under-represented and how this could be remedied. However, the solution is not only about those who are single. This issue cannot be detached from other areas of church life and culture.

Even though this is how the matter might best be addressed, this book is not aimed at achieving the entire outcome but only to make a small contribution toward the outcome.

Closing Reflections

If the discussion of this book contributes to the broader conversation, thereby raising awareness, broadening the outlook or helping in any small way to ensure that single people are not excluded from the fullness of the life of the community of God's people, then it will have fulfilled what it set out to achieve.

Appendix

National Church Life Survey 2023

Singleness, Marriage & being God's Family

Australian singles: A church and community comparison

Fleur Hourihan

March 2023

NCLS Research
PO Box 92
North Ryde BC NSW 1670
(p) +61 2 9139 2525
(e) info@ncls.org.au
(w) www.ncls.org.au

Appendix

Contents

1. Introduction 3
2. Methodology 3
3. Trends over time in the Australian Census 4
3.1 Singleness in the Australian population, 1954-2021 4
3.2 Religious affiliation in the Australian population, 1901-2021 5
4. Singleness in Australian churches, 1991-2021 6
5. Singleness: A comparison between church and community in 2021 9
5.1 Registered marital status 9
5.2 Social marital status 11
Data file references 14

List of tables

Table 1: Registered marital statuses of Australian population 15 years and over, 1954-2021 4
Table 2: Registered marital statuses of Australian population 25 years and over, 2011-2021 4
Table 3: Major religious affiliations of the Australian population, 1901-2021 5
Table 4: Marital statuses of Australian church attenders 25 years and over, 1991-2021 6
Table 5: Marital statuses of Australian church attenders, 15-24 years old 6
Table 6: Marital statuses of Australian church attenders, 25-34 years old 7
Table 7: Marital statuses of Australian church attenders, 35-44 years old 7
Table 8: Marital statuses of Australian church attenders, 45-54 years old 7
Table 9: Marital statuses of Australian church attenders, 55-64 years old 8
Table 10: Marital statuses of Australian church attenders, 65 years and over 8
Table 11: Marital statuses of Australian church attenders 25 years and over, by gender 8
Table 12: Marital statuses of Australian church attenders 25 years and over, by denomination type 9
Table 13: 2021 Registered marital statuses of Australians and Australian church attenders 25 years and over 10
Table 14: 2021 Registered marital statuses of Australians and Australian church attenders, 15-24 years old 10
Table 15: 2021 Registered marital statuses of Australians and Australian church attenders, 25-34 years old 10
Table 16: 2021 Registered marital statuses of Australians and Australian church attenders, 35-44 years old 10
Table 17: 2021 Registered marital statuses of Australians and Australian church attenders, 45-54 years old 11
Table 18: 2021 Registered marital statuses of Australians and Australian church attenders, 55-64 years old 11
Table 19: 2021 Registered marital statuses of Australians and Australian church attenders, 65 years and over 11
Table 20: 2021 Social marital statuses of Australians and Australian church attenders 25 years and over 12
Table 21: 2021 Social marital statuses of Australians and Australian church attenders, 15-24 years old 12
Table 22: 2021 Social marital statuses of Australians and Australian church attenders, 25-34 years old 12
Table 23: 2021 Social marital statuses of Australians and Australian church attenders, 35-44 years old 12
Table 24: 2021 Social marital statuses of Australians and Australian church attenders, 45-54 years old 13
Table 25: 2021 Social marital statuses of Australians and Australian church attenders, 55-64 years old 13
Table 26: 2021 Social marital statuses of Australians and Australian church attenders, 65 years and over 13

Citation

Hourihan, F. (2023) Australian singles: A church and community comparison. Sydney: NCLS Research.

Singleness, Marriage & being God's Family

1 Introduction

With singleness on the rise in Australian society, ensuring singles are not excluded from the life of the Church is an issue of great importance. When it comes to their marital statuses, are church attenders reflective of trends in wider Australian society? Are certain demographics, such as singles, under- or overrepresented in the pews?

Data from the 2021 National Church Life Survey, in conjunction with the 2021 Census of Population and Housing, presents a unique opportunity to compare the marital statuses of Australian church attenders with those of the Australian population, with a particular focus on singleness. This report firstly presents results on the marital statuses of the Australian population over time, using current and historical Census data. An overview is also given of how religious affiliation has changed in Australia over time. It then looks at marital status among Australian church attenders over time, including breakdowns by age, gender and denomination. Lastly, the report then provides a side-by-side comparison of 2021 NCLS and Census results on marital status.

2 Methodology

NCLS Research is a joint project of several denominational partners. Established in the early 1990s, it is a world leader in research focused on connecting churches and their communities. The most well-known project is the five-yearly National Church Life Survey (NCLS).

The NCLS is a quantitative survey of 150,000 to 450,000 church attenders, 6,000-10,000 church leaders and 3,000-7,000 churches in more than 20 Australian denominations (Catholic, Anglican and all the major Protestant) every census year since 1991. The survey covers a wide range of areas of religious faith and practice and social concern. The NCLS includes three major survey types:
1. Attender Surveys (comprising a main survey variant and multiple small sample survey variants);
2. Several variants of a Leader Survey which is completed by local church leaders; and
3. A church census survey of local church operations and activities.

This report presents Attender Survey results from 2021, based on survey forms returned by 128,480 respondents. The survey was available on paper and online. The completion period was extended well into 2022 to minimise the impact of the COVID pandemic and other events on church participation in the survey. Due to differing levels of participation in the survey across each denomination, the data were weighted according to the estimated total attendance of each denomination, to ensure that the overall statistics reflect as accurately as possible the actual distribution of attenders across the denominations. By weighting the data, a reliable picture of attenders in a typical week can be obtained.

Attenders from 19 denominations and movements were sampled well enough in 2021 to be included in the weighted analysis. These denominations/movements account for some 95% of the weekly church attenders in Australia (not including Orthodox, independent or house churches). The 19 denominations have been combined into larger groups in this report as follows:
1. Catholic
2. Mainstream Protestant (Anglican, Lutheran, Presbyterian, Uniting Church)
3. Pentecostal (Acts 2 Alliance, Acts Global, Australian Christian Churches, C3 Australia, CityLife Church, CRC Churches International, Hillsong Australia, International Network of Churches (INC))
4. Other Protestant (Baptist, Christian Reformed Church, Churches of Christ, Fellowship of Independent Evangelical Churches (FIEC), Salvation Army, Vineyard Churches Australia)

Appendix

3 Trends over time in the Australian Census

3.1 Singleness in the Australian population, 1954-2021

The proportion of single people in the Australian population has risen steadily since 1954. The Australian Census of Population and Housing (1971 onwards), and before that the Australian Commonwealth census, provide historical national data on the registered marital statuses of the Australian population. Table 1 shows census data from 1954-2021, for people aged 15 and over.

In 2021, over a third of Australians 15 years and over had never been married (37%), compared to just over a quarter in 1954 (26%). The proportion of singles in the population started consistently rising from 1981 onwards, and since then has shown little sign of plateauing. Corresponding with this upward trend of singleness is the downward trend of married Australians, dropping from 64.1% of the population in 1954 to 46.5% in 2021. In fact, Australians 15 years and over in registered marriages have been in the minority since 2006 (49.6% of the population).

Australians who are separated, divorced or widowed and haven't remarried may also be considered 'single'. The proportion of Australians who at the time of the census were separated from their spouse has risen slightly since 1954 (from 1.9% to 3.2%), while the proportion who were divorced has risen substantially (from 1.1% to 8.8%). The proportion of widowed Australians has decreased from 7.2% in 1954 to 5.0% in 2021, which can likely be attributed to advances in health care and rising life expectancies.

Table 1: Registered marital statuses of Australian population 15 years and over, 1954-2021

	1954 %	1961 %	1966 %	1971 %	1976 %	1981 %	1986 %	1991 %	1996 %	2001 %	2006 %	2011 %	2016 %	2021 %
Never married	25.7	25.5	26.3	24.9	25.0	26.8	28.4	29.3	30.5	31.6	33.2	34.3	35.0	36.5
Married	64.1	64.2	63.4	64.5	63.3	60.1	57.8	56.2	53.3	51.4	49.6	48.7	48.1	46.5
Separated	1.9	2.0	2.0	2.0	2.5	2.5	2.6	2.9	3.4	3.4	3.1	3.0	3.2	3.2
Divorced	1.1	1.1	1.2	1.5	2.2	3.7	4.7	5.3	6.4	7.4	8.2	8.4	8.5	8.8
Widowed	7.2	7.2	7.2	7.1	6.9	6.8	6.5	6.3	6.4	6.2	5.9	5.5	5.2	5.0

Source: 2021 Census of Population and Housing; 2016 Census of Population and Housing; 2011 Census of Population and Housing; ABS 3105.0.65.001 Australian Historical Population Statistics, 2008.

Table 2 excludes the youngest Australians from the results presented in Table 1, looking only at those aged 25 years or older. While the majority of this population in 2021 were currently in a registered marriage (54%), just over a quarter had never been married (26%), and one in ten were divorced.

Table 2: Registered marital statuses of Australian population 25 years and over, 2011-2021

	2011 %	2016 %	2021 %
Never married	22.1	23.6	26.0
Married	57.7	56.4	54.1
Separated but not divorced	3.6	3.8	3.8
Divorced	10.1	10.1	10.3
Widowed	6.5	6.1	5.8

Source: 2021 Census of Population and Housing; 2016 Census of Population and Housing; 2011 Census of Population and Housing.

A phenomenon that goes hand-in-hand with this rising singleness is that Australians are choosing to marry at an older age. In 1977, the median age of men at marriage (whether or not it was their first marriage) was 25.2 years, and the median age of women was 22.5 years. These ages have risen to 32.1 years for men and 30.5 years for women in 2021. This lends some

explanation as to why the proportion of singles in the population has grown since 1954 years, although various other socio-cultural factors are also likely at play.

3.2 Religious affiliation in the Australian population, 1901-2021

Another interesting trend from historical Census data is the change of religious affiliation in the Australian population over time. Table 3 details the major categories of religious affiliation as captured by the Australian Census since 1901. In the time span of over a century, the question wording, category definitions and ordering of question options has seen changes to the religion question asked in the Census, which inevitability is reflected in the data captured, somewhat affecting comparability over time. Even so, Table 3 demonstrates some very clear trends within Australian society when it comes to religion. The proportion of the population affiliating with no religion has grown substantially, up to 39% in 2021, while those who affiliate with Christianity (no matter the denomination) represented just under half of the population (44%) in 2021.

Table 3: Major religious affiliations of the Australian population, 1901-2021

Census year	Christianity				Other religions	No religion[b]	Not stated/ inadequately described	Total '000
	Anglican	Catholic	Other	Total				
1901	39.7	22.7	33.7	96.1	1.4	0.4	2.0	3773.8
1911	38.4	22.4	35.1	95.9	0.8	0.4	2.9	4455.0
1921	43.7	21.7	31.6	96.9	0.7	0.5	1.9	5435.7
1933	38.7	19.6	28.1	86.4	0.4	0.2	12.9	6629.8
1947	39.0	20.9	28.1	88.0	0.5	0.3	11.1	7579.4
1954	37.9	22.9	28.5	89.4	0.6	0.3	9.7	8986.5
1961	34.9	24.9	28.4	88.3	0.7	0.4	10.7	10508.2
1966	33.5	26.2	28.5	88.2	0.7	0.8	10.3	11599.5
1971	31.0	27.0	28.2	86.2	0.8	6.7	6.2	12755.6
1976	27.7	25.7	25.2	78.6	1.0	8.3	11.4	13548.4
1981	26.1	26.0	24.3	76.4	1.4	10.8	11.4	14576.3
1986	23.9	26.0	23.0	73.0	2.0	12.7	12.4	15602.2
1991	23.8	27.3	22.9	74.0	2.6	12.9	10.5	16850.3
1996	22.0	27.0	21.9	70.9	3.5	16.6	9.0	17752.8
2001	20.7	26.6	20.7	68.0	4.9	15.5	11.7	18769.2
2006	18.7	25.8	19.3	63.9	5.6	18.7	11.9	19855.3
2011[a]	17.1	25.3	18.7	61.1	7.2	22.3	9.3	21507.7
2016	13.3	22.6	16.3	52.1	8.2	30.1	9.6	23401.9
2021	9.8	20.0	14.1	43.9	1.3[c]	38.9	7.3	25422..8

[a] 2011 data has been calculated using the 2016 definitions.
[b] No religion includes secular beliefs (e.g. Atheism) and other spiritual beliefs (e.g. New Age).
[c] Other religions includes Australian Aboriginal Traditional Religions, Sikhism and other religious groups as defined in 2021
Sources: 2021 ABS Census of Population and Housing, ABS Census of Population and Housing, 2016 and historical.

Appendix

4 Singleness in Australian churches, 1991-2021

Church attenders from all seven NCLS survey waves (1991, 1996, 2001, 2006, 2011, 2016 and 2021) were asked about their marital status. This section examines how the marital statuses of church attenders have changed over time, using NCLS data that has been weighted to best represent the Australian church-going population.

A note on changes to question wording: From 2001 onwards, married attenders could select one of three options – 'In first marriage', 'Remarried after divorce', and 'Remarried after death of spouse'. In the survey years before this, there was only one option representing 'married'. Thus for the purposes of this analysis, the percentages shown for 'married' in 2001, 2006, 2011, 2016 and 2021 were calculated by adding the percentages from these three question options. Also, 'In a de facto relationship' was introduced as an option in the marital status question from 2001 onwards.

Table 4: Marital statuses of Australian church attenders 25 years and over, 1991-2021

	1991 %	1996 %	2001 %	2006 %	2011 %	2016 %	2021 %
Never married	8.7	8.7	9.0	9.3	10.3	9.4	10.1
Married	74.6	73.7	74.3	72.8	71.4	71.2	70.8
Separated but not divorced	1.8	2.0	1.8	1.7	1.8	1.8	1.7
Divorced	3.8	4.4	4.2	4.8	4.8	5.2	5.4
Widowed	11.2	11.3	9.9	10.4	10.3	10.6	10.4
De facto relationship*	NA	NA	0.9	1.0	1.4	1.8	1.7

Source: 2021 NCLS Attender Survey (n= 101,009) 2016 NCLS Attender Survey (n = 143,423), 2011 NCLS Attender Survey (n = 185,899), 2006 NCLS Attender Survey (n = 264,640), 2001 NCLS Attender Survey (n = 310,431), 1996 NCLS Attender Survey (n = 471,090), 1991 NCLS Attender Survey (n = 519,206). * 'In a de facto relationship' was introduced as an option in this question from 2001.

As shown in Table 4, the proportion of those 25 years and older in the Australian churchgoing population who have never married has remained fairly constant over the last 30 years, increasing by just over one percent between 1991 and 2021. The same can be said for the other marital statuses, which have also shown little change.

An examination of Tables 5-10 suggests that this overall stability masks some stronger trends occurring in certain age groups of church attenders. The proportion of those who had never married has risen in the past 30 years among attenders of all age groups except those 65 years and over, with the largest increase occurring among attenders 25-34 years old. While 22% of this age group in 1991 had never been married, this almost doubled, increasing to 41% in 2021 (with another 4% of this group in de facto relationships).

Table 5: Marital statuses of Australian church attenders, 15-24 years old

15-24 years old	1991 %	1996 %	2001 %	2006 %	2011 %	2016 %	2021 %
Never married	88.6	89.0	91.7	90.6	90.3	91.2	93.3
Married	10.8	10.5	6.7	7.4	7.4	6.7	5.0
Separated but not divorced	0.4	0.3	0.1	0.1	0.2	0.1	0.2
Divorced	0.2	0.1	0.1	0.1	0.2	0.2	0.0
Widowed	0.1	0.1	0.2	0.3	0.2	0.1	0.1
De facto relationship*	NA	NA	1.1	1.4	1.8	1.6	1.4

Source: 2021 NCLS Attender Survey (n = 6,628), 2016 NCLS Attender Survey (n = 13,588), 2011 NCLS Attender Survey (n = 21,410), 2006 NCLS Attender Survey (n = 30,652), 2001 NCLS Attender Survey (n = 36,686), 1996 NCLS Attender Survey (n = 63,638), 1991 NCLS Attender Survey (n = 77,218). * 'In a de facto relationship' was introduced as an option in this question from 2001.

Table 6: Marital statuses of Australian church attenders, 25-34 years old

25-34 years old	1991 %	1996 %	2001 %	2006 %	2011 %	2016 %	2021 %
Never married	22.2	26.2	30.7	34.3	36.1	33.0	40.9
Married	73.0	69.2	63.2	59.7	57.8	59.5	53.2
Separated but not divorced	2.0	2.0	1.5	1.3	1.0	1.3	0.6
Divorced	2.5	2.4	2.0	1.8	1.2	1.2	1.0
Widowed	0.3	0.2	0.2	0.2	0.1	0.3	0.0
De facto relationship*	NA	NA	2.4	2.7	3.7	4.8	4.2

Source: 2021 NCLS Attender Survey (n = 8,396), 2016 NCLS Attender Survey (n = 14,238), 2011 NCLS Attender Survey (n = 20,880), 2006 NCLS Attender Survey (n = 25,519), 2001 NCLS Attender Survey (n = 32,966), 1996 NCLS Attender Survey (n = 68,664), 1991 NCLS Attender Survey (n = 85,737). * 'In a de facto relationship' was introduced as an option in this question from 2001.

Table 7: Marital statuses of Australian church attenders, 35-44 years old

35-44 years old	1991 %	1996 %	2001 %	2006 %	2011 %	2016 %	2021 %
Never married	7.0	7.8	8.9	10.1	10.7	10.6	12.9
Married	84.6	83.3	82.5	81.1	80.5	80.5	80.0
Separated but not divorced	2.6	3.0	2.5	2.2	2.2	2.3	1.8
Divorced	4.9	5.2	4.2	4.6	4.0	3.5	2.6
Widowed	0.8	0.6	0.6	0.6	0.4	0.4	0.4
De facto relationship*	NA	NA	1.3	1.6	2.1	2.7	2.4

Source: 2021 NCLS Attender Survey (n = 12,733), 2016 NCLS Attender Survey (n = 19,454), 2011 NCLS Attender Survey (n = 26,113), 2006 NCLS Attender Survey (n = 40,205), 2001 NCLS Attender Survey (n = 55,778), 1996 NCLS Attender Survey (n = 94,991), 1991 NCLS Attender Survey (n = 109,611). * 'In a de facto relationship' was introduced as an option in this question from 2001.

Table 8: Marital statuses of Australian church attenders, 45-54 years old

45-54 years old	1991 %	1996 %	2001 %	2006 %	2011 %	2016 %	2021 %
Never married	4.6	4.7	6.0	6.8	8.1	8.2	8.4
Married	85.1	83.9	82.8	81.8	79.6	79.8	80.6
Separated but not divorced	2.3	2.9	2.7	2.5	3.2	2.7	2.7
Divorced	5.6	6.5	5.9	6.3	5.9	5.9	5.2
Widowed	2.5	2.1	1.7	1.6	1.7	1.3	1.0
De facto relationship*	NA	NA	1.0	1.1	1.6	2.2	2.0

Source: 2021 NCLS Attender Survey (n = 14,734), 2016 NCLS Attender Survey (n = 22,261), 2011 NCLS Attender Survey (n = 31,681), 2006 NCLS Attender Survey (n = 48,436), 2001 NCLS Attender Survey (n = 62,712), 1996 NCLS Attender Survey (n = 92,159), 1991 NCLS Attender Survey (n = 95,981). * 'In a de facto relationship' was introduced as an option in this question from 2001.

Appendix

Table 9: Marital statuses of Australian church attenders, 55-64 years old

55-64 years old	1991 %	1996 %	2001 %	2006 %	2011 %	2016 %	2021 %
Never married	5.1	4.5	5.1	5.6	6.7	6.9	7.7
Married	80.0	80.7	81.6	79.8	78.1	77.6	77.0
Separated but not divorced	1.5	1.7	1.8	1.9	2.2	2.3	2.5
Divorced	4.2	5.9	5.3	6.8	7.4	7.6	7.8
Widowed	9.1	7.2	5.5	4.9	4.5	4.0	3.2
De facto relationship*	NA	NA	0.6	0.9	1.1	1.5	1.8

Source: 2021 NCLS Attender Survey (n = 16,594), 2016 NCLS Attender Survey (n = 25,935), 2011 NCLS Attender Survey (n = 36,516), 2006 NCLS Attender Survey (n = 54,871), 2001 NCLS Attender Survey (n = 60,580), 1996 NCLS Attender Survey (n = 76,813), 1991 NCLS Attender Survey (n = 86,924). * 'In a de facto relationship' was introduced as an option in this question from 2001.

Table 10: Marital statuses of Australian church attenders, 65 years and over

65 years and over	1991 %	1996 %	2001 %	2006 %	2011 %	2016 %	2021 %
Never married	6.7	5.6	6.1	5.7	5.5	5.1	5.4
Married	57.3	58.6	63.4	64.3	65.0	65.1	66.3
Separated but not divorced	0.8	0.8	0.9	1.0	1.1	1.2	1.3
Divorced	2.2	2.6	3.0	3.8	4.4	5.4	6.1
Widowed	33.1	32.4	26.3	24.8	23.5	22.4	20.0
De facto relationship*	NA	NA	0.2	0.4	0.5	0.7	0.9

Source: 2021 NCLS Attender Survey (n = 48,552), 2016 NCLS Attender Survey (n = 61,534), 2011 NCLS Attender Survey (n = 72,431), 2006 NCLS Attender Survey (n = 95,610), 2001 NCLS Attender Survey (n = 98,395), 1996 NCLS Attender Survey (n = 138,465), 1991 NCLS Attender Survey (n = 140,953). * 'In a de facto relationship' was introduced as an option in this question from 2001.

Table 11 shows the gender breakdown of church attenders' marital statuses (25 years and older) over the 7 survey waves. In each year, male attenders were more likely to be currently married than female attenders. These differences are likely related to the significantly higher proportion of women attenders who are widowed or divorced; the gender difference is much smaller when looking at the proportion of attenders who had never been married.

Table 11: Marital statuses of Australian church attenders 25 years and over, by gender

	1991		1996		2001		2006		2011		2016		2021	
	% M	% F	% M	% F	% M	% F	% M	% F	% M	% F	% M	% F	% M	% F
Never married	9.3	8.4	9.5	8.2	9.6	8.6	9.7	9.3	9.7	9.0	10.6	10.2	9.7	10.2
Married	84.0	69.8	82.7	68.2	82.0	69.6	79.6	65.8	81.1	67.6	79.5	66.1	79.4	65.2
Separated	1.4	2.0	1.6	2.2	1.4	2.0	1.4	2.0	1.3	1.9	1.5	2.0	1.4	1.9
Divorced	2.5	4.6	3.0	5.3	2.7	5.0	3.2	6.4	3.1	5.9	3.2	5.8	3.3	6.7
Widowed	2.9	15.2	3.3	16.1	3.3	13.9	4.2	14.8	3.6	14.6	3.8	14.5	4.2	14.3
De facto relationship*	NA	NA	NA	NA	0.9	0.8	1.9	1.7	1.1	1.0	1.5	1.4	1.8	1.7

Source: 2021 NCLS Attender Survey (n = 100,207), 2016 NCLS Attender Survey (n = 141,991), 2011 NCLS Attender Survey (n = 182,537), 2006 NCLS Attender Survey (n = 259,284), 2001 NCLS Attender Survey (n = 304,873), 1996 NCLS Attender Survey (n = 464,964), 1991 NCLS Attender Survey (n = 487,761). *·'In a de facto relationship' was introduced as an option in this question from 2001.

Singleness, Marriage & being God's Family

Table 12 shows attenders' marital status in 2021 for each denominational grouping, compared with data from the 2001 NCLS (the earliest survey with an equivalent marital status question to 2021, i.e. including the 'de facto' option).

Table 12: Marital statuses of Australian church attenders 25 years and over, by denomination type

	Catholic		Mainstream Protestant		Pentecostal		Other Protestant	
	2001 %	2021 %	2001 %	2021 %	2001 %	2021 %	2001 %	2021 %
Never married	9.0	10.2	7.9	9.1	12.2	12.4	9.5	9.1
Married	75.3	68.7	72.0	69.5	72.7	73.8	75.9	75.1
Separated	1.7	1.8	1.5	1.3	3.1	2.1	2.1	1.5
Divorced	3.4	4.5	4.1	5.4	7.6	6.9	5.1	6.3
Widowed	9.7	12.4	13.7	13.3	3.6	3.4	6.9	7.2
De facto relationship	1.0	2.3	0.8	1.4	0.8	1.2	0.6	0.8

Source: 2021 NCLS Attender Survey (n = 101,009), 2001 NCLS Attender Survey (n = 310,431). The denominations each grouping consisted of for 2021 data can be found in the Methodology section. For 2001, they were as follows: Mainstream Protestant = Anglican, Lutheran, Presbyterian, Uniting; Pentecostal = Apostolic, Aust. Christian Churches, C3 Church, Christian Revival Crusade; Other Protestant = Adventist, Baptist, Bethesda, Churches of Christ, Christian Reformed, Missionary Alliance, Nazarene, Salvation Army, Vineyard Fellowship, Wesleyan Methodist, and Other.

Pentecostal attenders were more likely than those from other denominational groupings to have never been married, with 12% in 2021. This is likely related to their younger age profile than that of other denominations, which is also evident in the lower proportion of Pentecostals who are widowed (3%), compared especially with Mainstream Protestants (13%) and Catholics (12%). This grouping also has the highest proportion of attenders who are divorced (7%). Although none of the denominational groupings have seen great levels of change in the marital statuses of their attenders in the 20 years between 2001 and 2021, some slight changes are evident, such as the decline in Catholic attenders who are married from 75% to 69%.

5 Singleness: A comparison between church and community in 2021

So far this report has separately outlined the rates of singleness in the Australian population and church-going population, but how do the two compare? This section looks more closely at both the registered and social marital statuses of the Australian population as collected by the Australian Census, and how these compare with church attenders.

5.1 Registered marital status

Technical note: In order to align results from the NCLS and Census as far as possible and maximise comparability, 2021 NCLS percentages for marital status have been recalculated in this section to exclude the 'De facto relationship' option, which is not a category in the Census question on Registered Marital Status (de facto marriages are instead part of a separate Census question on Social Marital Status). This is why 20121 NCLS results in this section differ slightly from those presented in Section 4.

Table 13 shows that people 25 years and over who have never been married are underrepresented in Australian churches, making up 10.3% of the church-going population compared to 26.0% of the Australian population. A greater proportion of church attenders are in registered marriages – almost three quarters of attenders (72.0%) compared with 54.1% of all Australians 25 years and over. By the same token, those who are widowed are overrepresented in Australian churches, while people who are separated or divorced are underrepresented.

Appendix

Table 13: 2021 Registered marital statuses of Australians and Australian church attenders 25 years and over

	2021 Australian population			2021 Australian church attenders		
	% M	% F	% Total	% M	% F	% Total
Never married	28.9	23.3	**26.0**	10.0	10.4	**10.3**
Married	56.0	52.4	**54.1**	80.9	66.3	**72.0**
Separated	3.6	4.0	**3.8**	1.4	1.9	**1.7**
Divorced	8.9	11.6	**10.3**	3.3	6.8	**5.5**
Widowed	2.7	8.7	**5.8**	4.3	14.5	**10.5**

Source: ABS data; 2021 NCLS Attender Survey (n = 98,530).

For all age groups except those over 65 years old who were female, church attenders were less likely to have never been married than the wider Australian population (see Tables 14-19). This shows that the lower singles rates in churches are not simply due to the older age profile of their attenders, as this is a trend that exists within younger age groups as well.

Table 14: 2021 Registered marital statuses of Australians and Australian church attenders, 15-24 years old

15-24 years old	2021 Australian population			2021 Australian church attenders		
	% M	% F	% Total	% M	% F	% Total
Never married	98.5	96.9	**97.7**	95.2	94.1	**94.6**
Married	1.3	2.7	**2.0**	4.7	5.5	**5.1**
Separated	0.1	0.2	**0.1**	0.0	0.2	**0.2**
Divorced	<0.1	0.1	**0.1**	0.0	0.0	**0.0**
Widowed	<0.1	<0.1	**<0.1**	0.0	0.1	**0.1**

Source: ABS data; 2021 NCLS Attender Survey (n = 6,461).

Table 15: 2021 Registered marital statuses of Australians and Australian church attenders, 25-34 years old

25-34 years old	2021 Australian population			2021 Australian church attenders		
	% M	% F	% Total	% M	% F	% Total
Never married	68.5	58.2	**63.3**	44.7	41.3	**42.7**
Married	28.7	37.2	**33.0**	54.2	56.5	**55.5**
Separated	1.3	2.2	**1.8**	0.5	0.8	**0.7**
Divorced	1.4	2.3	**1.8**	0.6	1.4	**1.1**
Widowed	0.1	0.1	**0.1**	0.0	0.0	**0.0**

Source: ABS data; 2021 NCLS Attender Survey (n = 7,989).

Table 16: 2021 Registered marital statuses of Australians and Australian church attenders, 35-44 years old

35-44 years old	2021 Australian population			2021 Australian church attenders		
	% M	% F	% Total	% M	% F	% Total
Never married	31.0	26.4	**28.7**	11.9	14.1	**13.2**
Married	60.0	60.9	**60.4**	85.5	79.6	**82.0**

NCLS Research
E: info@ncls.org.au, Tel: 02 9139 2525, W: www.ncls.org.au
Post: PO Box 92, North Ryde BC NSW 1670

© Copyright 2023 NCLS Research

Separated	3.5	4.7	**4.1**	1.2	2.2	**1.8**
Divorced	5.3	7.4	**6.4**	1.3	3.4	**2.6**
Widowed	0.2	0.6	**0.4**	0.1	0.6	**0.4**

Source: ABS data; 2021 NCLS Attender Survey (n = 12,320).

Table 17: 2021 Registered marital statuses of Australians and Australian church attenders, 45-54 years old

45-54 years old	2021 Australian population			2021 Australian church attenders		
	% M	% F	% Total	% M	% F	% Total
Never married	22.4	18.4	**20.4**	7.3	9.5	**8.6**
Married	61.1	59.3	**60.2**	86.6	79.5	**82.3**
Separated	5.0	5.9	**5.6**	2.1	3.3	**2.8**
Divorced	10.8	14.7	**12.8**	3.7	6.4	**5.3**
Widowed	0.6	1.7	**1.2**	0.3	1.4	**1.0**

Source: ABS data; 2021 NCLS Attender Survey (n = 14,289).

Table 18: 2021 Registered marital statuses of Australians and Australian church attenders, 55-64 years old

55-64 years old	2021 Australian population			2021 Australian church attenders		
	% M	% F	% Total	% M	% F	% Total
Never married	15.6	11.5	**13.5**	8.1	7.5	**7.7**
Married	63.0	59.1	**61.0**	84.4	74.5	**78.5**
Separated	4.8	5.1	**5.0**	1.9	3.0	**2.6**
Divorced	15.0	19.2	**17.1**	4.5	10.2	**7.9**
Widowed	1.6	5.1	**3.4**	1.1	4.7	**3.3**

Source: ABS data; 2021 NCLS Attender Survey (n = 16,192).

Table 19: 2021 Registered marital statuses of Australians and Australian church attenders, 65 years and over

65 years and over	2021 Australian population			2021 Australian church attenders		
	% M	% F	% Total	% M	% F	% Total
Never married	6.9	4.9	**5.8**	4.7	5.9	**5.4**
Married	67.5	48.5	**57.4**	81.6	58.0	**66.9**
Separated	3.6	2.7	**3.1**	1.3	1.2	**1.3**
Divorced	12.7	14.9	**13.9**	3.8	7.6	**6.2**
Widowed	9.3	29.1	**19.9**	8.6	27.3	**20.3**

Source: ABS data; 2021 NCLS Attender Survey (n = 47,740).

5.2 Social marital status

Technical note: For the purposes of comparing NCLS and Census results, the NCLS marital status survey question options have been recoded into the three Census categories for Social Marital Status as follows: 'Married in a registered marriage' = 'In first marriage', 'Remarried after divorced', 'Remarried after widowed'; 'Married in a de facto marriage' = 'In a de facto relationship'; 'Not married' = 'Never married', 'Separated', 'Divorced', 'Widowed'.

Note that Census results for 'Married in a registered marriage' in Tables 20-26 are not identical to Census results for 'Married' in Tables 13-19, because results were derived from separate questions in the Census with different response rates and calculations involved.

Appendix

Table 20 shows that church attenders 25 years and over are less likely to be single than the wider Australian population (27.6% versus 33.6%). This difference in social marital status between the two populations is smaller than when only registered marriages are considered, given that de facto marriages are much more prevalent in the wider population than among church attenders (12.2% versus 1.7%).

Table 20: 2021 Social marital statuses of Australians and Australian church attenders 25 years and over

	2021 Australian population			2021 Australian church attenders		
	% M	% F	% Total	% M	% F	% Total
Married in a registered marriage	56.1	52.5	**54.2**	79.4	65.2	**70.8**
Married in a de facto marriage	12.8	11.6	**12.2**	1.8	1.6	**1.7**
Not married	31.1	36.0	**33.6**	18.8	33.1	**27.6**

Source: ABS data; 2021 NCLS Attender Survey (n = 100,207).

For all age groups except those aged 15-24 years, the general population were more likely to be 'Not married' than church attenders (see Tables 21-26). This difference was largest for 45-54 year olds, with 28.6% of the Australian population not in a registered or de facto marriage compared with 17.3% of church attenders. Across all age groups, a much lower proportion of attenders were involved in de facto relationships/marriages than the general population. While one in four Australians aged 25-34 years old were in a de facto marriage (24.5%), just 4.2% of church attenders of the same age group fit this category. However, the distribution was similar between the two groups – de facto marriages peaked in frequency in the 25-34 year age range and then steadily became less common as age increased.

Table 21: 2021 Social marital statuses of Australians and Australian church attenders, 15-24 years old

15-24 years old	2021 Australian population			2021 Australian church attenders		
	% M	% F	% Total	% M	% F	% Total
Married in a registered marriage	1.0	2.4	**1.7**	4.6	5.4	**5.0**
Married in a de facto marriage	6.2	9.7	**7.9**	1.4	1.4	**1.4**
Not married	92.8	88.0	**90.4**	93.8	93.1	**93.5**

Source: ABS data; 2021 NCLS Attender Survey (n = 6,555).

Table 22: 2021 Social marital statuses of Australians and Australian church attenders, 25-34 years old

25-34 years old	2021 Australian population			2021 Australian church attenders		
	% M	% F	% Total	% M	% F	% Total
Married in a registered marriage	27.7	36.8	**32.3**	52.1	53.9	**53.2**
Married in a de facto marriage	24.3	24.6	**24.5**	3.7	4.5	**4.2**
Not married	48.0	38.6	**43.2**	44.1	41.4	**42.5**

Source: ABS data; 2021 NCLS Attender Survey (n = 8,338).

Table 23: 2021 Social marital statuses of Australians and Australian church attenders, 35-44 years old

35-44 years old	2021 Australian population			2021 Australian church attenders		
	% M	% F	% Total	% M	% F	% Total
Married in a registered marriage	60.0	60.9	**60.5**	83.7	77.7	**80.1**
Married in a de facto marriage	14.7	13.3	**14.0**	2.2	2.4	**2.3**
Not married	25.3	25.7	**25.5**	14.1	19.9	**17.6**

Singleness, Marriage & being God's Family

Source: ABS data; 2021 NCLS Attender Survey (n = 12,615).

Table 24: 2021 Social marital statuses of Australians and Australian church attenders, 45-54 years old

45-54 years old	2021 Australian population			2021 Australian church attenders		
	% M	% F	% Total	% M	% F	% Total
Married in a registered marriage	61.6	59.0	60.3	85.2	77.6	80.6
Married in a de facto marriage	11.7	10.5	11.1	1.6	2.3	2.0
Not married	26.7	30.4	28.6	13.3	20.1	17.3

Source: ABS data; 2021 NCLS Attender Survey (n = 14,586).

Table 25: 2021 Social marital statuses of Australians and Australian church attenders, 55-64 years old

55-64 years old	2021 Australian population			2021 Australian church attenders		
	% M	% F	% Total	% M	% F	% Total
Married in a registered marriage	63.0	58.3	60.6	82.9	73.3	77.0
Married in a de facto marriage	9.1	7.6	8.3	1.8	1.7	1.8
Not married	27.8	34.2	31.1	15.3	25.0	21.1

Source: ABS data; 2021 NCLS Attender Survey (n = 16,481).

Table 26: 2021 Social marital statuses of Australians and Australian church attenders, 65 years and over

65 years and over	2021 Australian population			2021 Australian church attenders		
	% M	% F	% Total	% M	% F	% Total
Married in a registered marriage	68.3	49.4	58.3	80.5	57.7	66.3
Married in a de facto marriage	4.7	3.0	3.8	1.3	0.7	0.9
Not married	27.1	47.6	37.9	18.2	41.6	32.9

Source: ABS data; 2021 NCLS Attender Survey (n = 48,185).

With more and more Australian adults finding themselves outside of marriage, it is crucial for churches to seek to engage single men and women, rather than only being family-oriented. NCLS data shows that singles – including those who have never married, or are separated or divorced – are underrepresented in Australian churches. These findings should prompt discussions about how to best make churches welcoming to people of all marital statuses.

Appendix

Data file references

Australian Bureau of Statistics (2006), *Year Book Australia, 2006, Religious Affiliation*, cat. no. 1301.0 (http://www.abs.gov.au/ausstats/abs@.nsf/46d1bc47ac9d0c7bca256c470025ff87/bfdda1ca506d6cfaca2570de0014496e!OpenDocument).

Australian Bureau of Statistics (2007), *Census shows non-Christian religions continue to grow at a faster rate*, cat. no. 2914.0.55.002 (http://www.abs.gov.au/ausstats/abs@.nsf/7d12b0f6763c78caca25706 1001cc588/6ef598989db79931ca257306000d52b4!OpenDocument).

Australian Bureau of Statistics (2008), 3105.0.65.001 Australian Historical Population Statistics.

Australian Bureau of Statistics (2012), *Marriages, de facto relationships and divorces*, cat. no. 1301.0 (http://www.abs.gov.au/ausstats/abs@.nsf/Lookup/by%20Subject/1301.0~2012~Main%20Features~Marriages,%20de%20facto%20relationships%20and%20divorces~55).

Australian Bureau of Statistics (2017), *Census 2016, Registered Marital Status by Age by Sex (SA2+)*, ABS.Stat, Dataset code ABS_C16_T02_SA (http://stat.data.abs.gov.au/index.aspx?DatasetCode=ABS_C16_T02_SA).

Australian Bureau of Statistics (2017), *Census 2016, Social Marital Status by Age by Sex (SA2+)*, ABS.Stat, Dataset code ABS_C16_T03_SA (http://stat.data.abs.gov.au/index.aspx?DatasetCode=ABS_C16_T03_SA).

Australian Bureau of Statistics (2017), *Census of Population and Housing: Reflecting Australia - Stories from the Census, 2016*, cat. no. 2071.0 (http://www.abs.gov.au/ausstats/abs@.nsf/Lookup/by%20Subject/2071.0~2016~Main%20Features~Religion%20Article~80).

Australian Bureau of Statistics (2017), *Marriages and Divorces, Australia*, cat. no. 3310.0 – 2016 (http://www.abs.gov.au/AUSSTATS/abs@.nsf/Lookup/3310.0Main+Features12016?OpenDocument).

Australian Bureau of Statistics. (2021). *Marriages and Divorces, Australia*. ABS. (https://www.abs.gov.au/statistics/people/people-and-communities/marriages-and-divorces-australia/latest-release.)

Australian Bureau of Statistics (2021), *Australia 2021 Census Community Profiles, General Community Profile, Australia* (https://abs.gov.au/census/find-census-data/community-profiles/2021/AUS)

Castle, K. (2001), 2001 NCLS Attender Survey A, [data file], NCLS Research, Sydney.

Castle, K. (2006), 2006 NCLS Attender Survey A, [data file], NCLS Research, Sydney.

Kaldor, P. (1991), 1991 NCLS Attender Survey A, [data file], NCLS Research, Sydney.

Kaldor, P. (1996), 1996 NCLS Attender Survey A, [data file], NCLS Research, Sydney.

Powell, R. (2011), 2011 NCLS Attender Survey A, [data file], NCLS Research, Sydney.

Powell, R., Pepper, M., Hancock, N., & Sterland, S. (2016), 2016 NCLS Attender Survey A, [data file], NCLS Research, Sydney.
Powell, R., Sterland, S., Gan, C., Pepper, M. & Hourihan, F. (2021). 2021 NCLS Attender Survey [data file]. NCLS Research, Sydney.

Notes

Introduction

1. Philip. B. Wilson (2005) *Being Single — Insights for Tomorrow's Church* (London, Darton, Longman and Todd) p182

2. Millard J. Erickson (2013) *Christian Theology* (3rd edn.). (Grand Rapids, MI, Baker Academic) p508

3. Andreas J. Köstenberger and David W. Jones (2010) *God, Marriage and Family: Rebuilding the Biblical Foundation* (2nd edn.). (Wheaton, IL, Crossway) p167

4. Kevin Andrews (2012) *Maybe 'I Do': Modern Marriage & the Pursuit of Happiness*. (Ballan, Vic., Connor Court Publishing) p1

5. Fleur Hourihan (2023) "Australian Singles – A Church and Community Comparison" (Sydney, National Church Life Survey [NCLS] Research), NCLS Report, Appendix p3, p13

6. Hourihan (2023) Appendix, NCLS Report, Table 3

7. *ibid*. Table 3

8. *ibid*. Table 1

Chapter 1

1. Wilson (2005) p182

2. *ibid*. p182

3. The summary and review of Philip B. Wilson's book *Being Single — Insights for Tomorrow's Church* in Chapter 1 follow the structure and order used in his book. This has been done with the copyright owner's permission.

4. Wilson (2005) p1
5. *ibid.* pp2-4, p24
6. *ibid.* p8
7. *ibid.* pp8-9
8. *ibid.* p10
9. *ibid.* p11
10. *ibid.* p12
11. *ibid.* pp12-13
12. *ibid.* p13
13. *ibid.* pp13-16
14. *ibid.* pp26-27
15. *ibid.* p27
16. *ibid.* pp16-17
17. John Bunyan (1678) *The Pilgrim's Progress* (reprint 1992, Belfast, Ambassador) p312; Wilson (2005) p17
18. Wilson (2005) p18
19. *ibid.* p18
20. *ibid.* pp19-20
21. *ibid.* pp19-20
22. Margo Todd (1987), *Christian Humanism and the Puritan Social Order* (Cambridge, Cambridge University Press) pp96f; Wilson (2005) p19
23. Aristotle. *The Politics, Book 1:3-13* (Cambridge, Cambridge University Press, 1988), p420; Wilson (2005) pp19-20
24. Wilson (2005) p20
25. *ibid.* pp20-21
26. *ibid.* p21
27. *ibid.* p36
28. *ibid.* p38
29. *ibid.* p29
30. *ibid.* p37

31. *ibid.* p37
32. *ibid.* p37
33. 3*ibid.* p30
34. *ibid.* p30
35. *ibid.* pp28-29
36. *ibid.* p29
37. *ibid.* pp36-60
38. *ibid.* pp50-54
39. *ibid.* p49
40. *ibid.* p50
41. *ibid.* pp55-57
42. *ibid.* p59
43. *ibid.* pp61-104
44. *ibid.* pp105-156
45. *ibid.* pp132-145
46. *ibid.* p147, p209
47. *ibid.* p151
48. *ibid.* p154
49. *ibid.* p165
50. *ibid.* p165
51. *ibid.* pp166-176
52. *ibid.* p167
53. Jonathan Sacks (1995) *Faith in the Future* (London, Darton, Longman and Todd) p29; Wilson (2005) pp167-169
54. Wilson (2005) p170
55. *ibid.* p171
56. *ibid.* p174
57. *ibid.* p174
58. *ibid.* pp182-201
59. *ibid.* p188

60. Stanley Hauerwas (1986) *A Community of Character* (Notre Dame, IN, University of Notre Dame) p189; Wilson (2005) p191
61. Wilson (2005) p182
62. *ibid.* pp197-198
63. *ibid.* p182

Chapter 2

1. see Hourihan (2023) Appendix, NCLS Report, Table 13
2. *ibid.* Tables 21-26
3. Wilson (2005) p167
4. *ibid.* p199
5. Andreas J. Köstenberger and David W. Jones (2010) *God, Marriage and Family: Rebuilding the Biblical Foundation* (2nd edn.) (Wheaton, IL, Crossway) p16
6. Andrews (2012) p9
7. see Hourihan (2023) Appendix, NCLS Report Table 1, Table 3
8. Wilson (2005) pp56-59.
9. *ibid.* p155
10. Köstenberger and Jones (2010) pp16-17
11. Hugh Mackay (1997) *Generations: Baby Boomers, Their Parents and Their Children* (Sydney, McMillan) pp118-119; Daniel Yankelovich (1994) "How changes in the economy are reshaping American values", in H. J. Aaron, T. E. Mann and T. Taylor (eds) *Values and Public Policy* (Washington DC, The Brookings Institute); Andrews (2012) p118
12. Mary Ann Glendon (2001) *A World Made New* (New York, NY, Random House); Andrews (2012) p118
13. Mackay (1997) pp118-119; Andrews (2012) p118
14. Andrews (2012) pp28-30
15. Andrews (2012) pp29-48, p97
16. *ibid.* p29
17. *ibid.* p142
18. *ibid.* pp137-139

19. Köstenberger and Jones (2010) pp15-17
20. Andrews (2012) pp119-122
21. Wilson (2005) pp49-51
22. *ibid.* p50
23. Andrews (2012) p119
24. Köstenberger and Jones (2010) p16
25. *ibid.* p16
26. Edmund Leach (1967) *A Runaway World?* (London, BBC [Reith Lectures]; Andrews (2012) p120
27. Wilson (2005) p51
28. Family Voice Australia (17 May 2021) "The natural family is under assault": https://familyvoice.org.au/news/the-natural-family-is-under-assault ; Canberra Declaration (n.d.), *'Freedom–Family–Faith–Life'*: https://canberradeclaration.org.au/; Canberra Declaration (2018) The Canberra Declaration: https://canberradeclaration.org.au/join-us/read-declaration/; Andrews (2012) p1, p352
29. National Families Week (2022) "About the week": https://nfw.org.au/about/; Family Voice Australia (17 May 2021) "The natural family is under assault": https://familyvoice.org.au/news/the-natural-family-is-under-assault ; Aristotle, p420; Wilson (2005) pp19-20
30. Andrews (2012) p19
31. *ibid.* p107
32. *ibid.* p353
33. *ibid.* p353
34. see *ibid.* p12, p107
35. see Chapter 6 for more discussion on the 'last Adam' and the 'first Adam'
36. Erickson 2013, p587

Chapter 3

1. Compelling Truth (2022) "What is the meaning of *phileo* love?" https://www.compellingtruth.org/phileo-love.html ; God's Word First (2010) "Defining love in the Bible": gods-word-first.org/fruitofspirit/biblelove-agape-phileo-eros-storge.html [for Greek definitions of love]

2. Wilson (2005) p49; Andrews (2012) p3, p5
3. Andrews (2012) pp119-122; Wilson (2005) pp49-51
4. R. C. Sproul (22 Jul 2019) "The most solemn mandate". *Biblical Wisdom for Parents:* https://biblical-parenting.org/articles/the-most-solemn-mandate/; Deut 6:4-9
5. see Dr A. Zimmermann (26 October 2018) *Christian Foundations of the Australian Law:* Western Australian Legal Theory Association. https://walta.net.au/2018/10/26/christian-foundations-of-the-australian-law/, p8.
6. Andrews (2012) p353
7. Families Australia (2022) "Events – National Families Week": https://familiesaustralia.org.au/events/national-families-week/
8. National Families Week (2022) "About the week" [embedded quote by Dr Brian Babington (2019)]: https://nfw.org.au/about/
9. see Canberra Declaration (2022) *Campaigns – Standing for Family:* https://canberradeclaration.org.au/campaigns/standing-for-family/; Greg Smalley (29 April 2021) "9 reasons to get married": https://www.families.org.au/article/9-reasons-get-married
10. e.g., see Andrews (2012) p353; Canberra Declaration (2022) *Campaigns – Standing for Family:* https://canberradeclaration.org.au/campaigns/standing-for-family/
11. Wilson (2005) pp19-20
12. Köstenberger and Jones (2010) p66, p183; National Families Week (2022) "About the week": https://nfw.org.au/about/
13. Joseph H. Hellerman (30 March 2016) "Our priorities are off when family is more important than church". *Christianity Today:* https://www.christianitytoday.com/ct/2016/august-web-only/if-our-families-are-mor-important-than-our-churches-we-nee.html
14. see Andrews (2012) p1, p354
15. see *Pulpit Commentary* (circa 1890s). Created under direction of Rev J. S. Exell and H. D. M. Spence-Jones (New York, NY, Toronto, Funk & Wagnalls), available at Bible Hub, *Online Bible Study Suite.* http://biblehub.com/commentaries/Genesis/1-22.htm
16. see Chapter 8 'Categories of biblical law' for more discussion on the relevance of God's moral law for us today.

17. Wilson (2005) pp19-20
18. see Andrews (2012) pp141-142, p348
19. see Canberra Declaration (2022) *Campaigns – Standing for Family:* https://canberradeclaration.org.au/campaigns/standing-for-family/; Arnold Toynbee [No reference is given here to the original source of the quote attributed to Arnold Toynbee, "Nations rise and fall with the health of its families". I could not find a citation for it on the Canberra Declaration website. When I contacted the Canberra Declaration office, they failed to respond to communication requesting a reference to the original source of the quote (email correspondence July/August and December 2022)].
20. Andrews (2012) p353

Chapter 4

1. Australian Government and Australian Institute of Family Studies (AIFS) (March 2022) *Marriages in Australia: Family Trends and Transitions.* Researchers: Lixia Qu, Jennifer Baxter and Megan Carroll: https://aifs.gov.au/facts-and-figures/marriages-australia
2. Figure 4.1 sourced from Australian Government and Australian Institute of Family Studies (AIFS) (March 2022) *Marriages in Australia: Family Trends and Transitions.* https://aifs.gov.au/research/facts-and-figures/marriages-australia. Used with permission of the copyright holder (AIFS on behalf of the Commonwealth of Australia) [see https://aifs.gov.au/main/copyright] and under the Creative Commons Licence [see https://creativecommons.org/licenses/by/4.0/]
3. Mikki Morrissette (2008) *Choosing Single Motherhood – The Thinking Woman's Guide* (Houghton Mifflin Harcourt); Jane Mattes (1994), *Single Mothers by Choice – A Guidebook for Single Women Who Are Considering or Have Chosen Motherhood* (Harmony)
4. see Andrews (2012) p353
5. Pope John Paul II (2000). Message to the Family: Dare to Dream Conference, Melbourne; Andrews (2012) p105
6. Canberra Declaration (2022) *Campaigns – Standing for Family:* canberradeclaration.org.au/campaigns/standing-for-family/; Margaret Mead [No reference is given here to the original source of the quote attributed to Margaret Mead, "As families go, so goes the nation". I could not find a citation for it on the Canberra Declaration website. When

I contacted the Canberra Declaration office, they failed to respond to communication requesting a reference to the original source of the quote (email correspondence July/August and December 2022)]

7. John Wesley (1754-1765) *Explanatory Notes of the Whole Bible:* biblehub.com/commentaries/wes/luke/14.htm
8. John Gill (1746-1763). *Exposition of the Entire Bible:* biblehub.com/commentaries/luke/14-26.htm
9. see Hourihan (2023) Appendix, NCLS Report
10. Wilson (2005) pp166-167
11. see Köstenberger and Jones (2010) p171, p198, p264
12. see Chapter 6 for further discussion on the 'last Adam' and the 'first Adam'

Chapter 5

1. 1Erickson (2013) p469
2. *ibid.* p458
3. *ibid.* pp461-462
4. *ibid.* p466
5. *ibid.* pp464-465
6. *ibid.* p458
7. *ibid.* pp471-472
8. *ibid.* pp471-472
9. John Wesley (1754-65): www.biblehub.com/commentaries/wes/Genesis/5.htm
10. 1Erickson (2013) p472
11. *ibid.* pp458-459
12. *ibid.* p459
13. *ibid.* p459
14. *ibid.* p460
15. *ibid.* pp463-465
16. *ibid.* p505
17. *ibid.* p464

18. Millard. J. Erickson (1994) *Christian Theology* (1st edn.) (Grand Rapids, MI, Baker Books) p505; Karl Barth (1958) *Church Dogmatics* (Edinburgh, T and T Clark) vol. 3, part 1, pp197-198
19. Erickson (2013) p467
20. *ibid.* p468
21. *ibid.* p466
22. *ibid.* p467
23. *ibid.* p469
24. *ibid.* p469
25. see Kostenberger and Jones (2010) pp23-24, p269
26. Erickson (2013) pp460-463
27. *ibid.* p461
28. *ibid.* p461
29. see Focus on the Family (12 May 2017) "God and Man as Male and Female: Implications for Gender Identity": https://www.focusonthefamily.com/family-qa/god-and-man-as-male-and-female-implications-for-gender-identity/
30. Paul Sands (Jan 2010). "The *Imago Dei* as vocation", *Evangelical Quarterly* 82(1), pp28-41
31. Paul Sands (Jan 2010). *Evangelical Quarterly* 82(1), p36
32. Erickson (2013) p469
33. see Focus on the Family (12 May 2017). "God and Man as Male and Female: Implications for Gender Identity"

Chapter 6

1. see Andrews (2012) pp353-354
2. Rev Joseph Benson (1857) *Commentary on the Old and New Testaments* (2nd edn. 1811-1818. Republished New York, NY, by T. Carlton and J. Porter); John Gill (1746-1763): both available at Bible Hub: https://biblehub.com/commentaries/acts/1-6.htm

Chapter 7

1. see Robert. H. Gundry (2010) *Commentary on the New Testament: Verse-by-Verse Explanations with a Literal Translation* (Peabody, MA, Hendrickson) p685
2. Wilson (2005) p168
3. Albert Barnes (1834) *Barnes' Notes on the Bible.* [Barnes 1798–1870]; John Gill (1746-1763): both available at Bible Hub: https://biblehub.com/commentaries/luke/1-25.htm
4. Kutter Callaway (2018) *Breaking the Marriage Idol: Reconstructing Our Cultural and Spiritual Norms* (Downers Grove, IL, Intervarsity Press) p113
5. Robert. H. Gundry (2010) p685
6. *Pulpit Commentary* (circa 1890s): https://biblehub.com/commentaries/Genesis/2-18.htm
7. see Köstenberger and Jones (2010) p171, p198, p264; Wilson (2005) pp166-167
8. e.g., see Köstenberger and Jones (2010) p36, p67, pp117-118, p125, p133
9. see *ibid.* p168, p171
10. David Prior (1985) *The Message of 1 Corinthians.* (London, Intervarsity Press), p108; Barry Danylak (2010) *Redeeming Singleness – How the Storyline of Scripture Affirms the Single Life* (Wheaton, IL, Crossway) p200; see Chapter 9 for further discussion on the concept of the 'gift of singleness'
11. e.g., see Köstenberger and Jones (2010) p36, p117
12. Albert Barnes (1834) https://biblehub.com/commentaries/barnes/isaiah/56.htm
13. John Gill (1746-1763): https://biblehub.com/commentaries/gill/isaiah/56.htm; Is 56:5
14. Gundry (2010) p748

Chapter 8

1. Köstenberger and Jones (2010) p15
2. Albert Barnes (1834); John Gill (1746-63): both available at Bible Hub: https://biblehub.com/commentaries/john/12-31.htm
3. Selwyn Hughes (Sat 5 Feb 2022) *Every Day with Jesus (EDWJ)* (Farnham, Surrey, Waverley Abbey Resources). Jan/Feb 2022.
4. Billy Graham Evangelistic Association (1 June 2004) "Which of the hundreds of Old Testament laws are applicable to us as Christians?" https://billygraham.org/answer/which-of-the-hundreds-of-old-testament-laws-are-applicable-to-us-as-christians/; J. D. Greear Ministries (30 March 2016) "Why don't we follow all of the Old Testament laws?" https://jdgreear.com/why-dont-we-follow-all-of-the-old-testament-laws/ [The categories of biblical law and the following paragraph on the explanation of their relevance today are taken from these sources].
5. see Hourihan (2023) Appendix, NCLS Report, Table 3; Australian Bureau of Statistics https://www.abs.gov.au/articles/religious-affiliation-australia
6. Hourihan, Appendix, NCLS Report, Table 3
7. Hugh Mackay (1997) pp118-119; Daniel Yankelovich (1994); Andrews (2012) p118
8. https://www.studylight.org/encyclopedias/eng/tje/h/holiness.html
9. Wilson (2005) p191, p 197
10. see Canberra Declaration (2010) *Key Signatories:* https://canberradeclaration.org.au/join-us/read-declaration/contributors/
11. Wilson (2005) p38
12. *ibid.* pp28-29
13. *ibid.* pp40-44
14. see Appendix, Table 1
15. see Appendix, Table 3
16. see Wilson (2005) pp56-59

Chapter 9

1. see Köstenberger and Jones (2010) p67, pp171-173
2. see *ibid.* p168, p171
3. see *ibid.* p171
4. Charles John Ellicott (n.d.) *Ellicott's Commentary for English Readers* (London, Cassell): www.biblehub.com/commentaries/1_corinthians/7-7.htm
5. Albert Barnes (1834): www.biblehub.com/commentaries/1_corinthians/7-7.htm
6. Matthew Poole (circa 1685) *Poole's Commentary;* John Gill (1746-1763); *Pulpit Commentary* (circa 1890s): all at Bible Hub: www.biblehub.com/commentaries/1_corinthians/7-7.htm
7. Heinrich August Wilhelm Meyer. (1883). *Commentary on the New Testament – Critical and Exegetical* (New York, NY, Funk & Wagnalls): www.biblehub.com/commentaries/1_corinthians/7-7.htm
8. see Köstenberger and Jones (2010) p168, pp171-172
9. Charles John Ellicott (n.d.): at www.biblehub.com/commentaries/matthew/19-11.htm
10. Paul Barnett (2011) *Focus on the Bible, 1 Corinthians – Holiness and Hope of a Rescued People* (Christian Focus Publications) p112
11. see Gundry (2010), p650; Prior (1985) p108; Danylak (2010) p200
12. Prior (1985) p108; Danylak (2010) p200
13. Danylak (2010) p200
14. *ibid.* pp200-201
15. see the account of Abraham's life in Chapter 6
16. see Danylak (2010) p201; Köstenberger and Jones (2010) p67, pp171-173
17. There are numerous websites available to find music by searching selected lyrics, and for searching lines used in movie dialogue, for example: Genius [world's biggest collection of song lyrics and music knowledge]: https://genius.com/ ; QuoDB. (n.d.) [find any quote in millions of movie lines]: https://www.quodb.com/

18. Alfred Lord Tennyson (1850) *In Memoriam A. H. H.* (London, Edward Moxon). [poem]
19. Bella DePaulo (17 Aug 2008) "Is it better to have loved and lost than never to have loved at all?" *Psychology Today,* Sussex Publishers, LLC: https://www.psychologytoday.com/us/blog/living-single/200808/is-it-better-have-loved-and-lost-never-have-loved-all
20. Albert Barnes (1834); John Gill (1746-1763): both available at Bible Hub: biblehub.com/commentaries/matthew/22-11.htm
21. Rev Joseph Benson (1857); C. J. Ellicott, *Ellicott's Commentary for English Readers* (n.d.); Matthew Henry (1706) *Concise Commentary on the Whole Bible.* (republished 1963, Chicago, IL, Moody Press); Robert Jamieson, A. R. Fausset and David Brown (1882) *A Commentary on the Old and New Testaments* (Toledo, OH, J. B. Names and Co.); Albert Barnes (1834); John Gill (1746-1763): all available at Bible Hub: biblehub.com/commentaries/matthew/22-11.htm
22. Hourihan (2023) Appendix, NCLS Report, Table 3
23. *New International Version [NIV] Study Bible* (1985) (Grand Rapids, MI, Zondervan), p860

Chapter 10

1. see Köstenberger and (Jones 2010) p259
2. Wilson (2005) pp166-167
3. *ibid.* p182
4. *ibid.* pp170-173
5. see Gundry (2010) p698
6. see Hourihan (2023) Appendix, NCLS Report, Table 1

Bibliography

Andrews, Kevin. (2012) *Maybe 'I Do': Modern Marriage & the Pursuit of Happiness* (Ballan, Vic., Connor Court Publishing).

Aristotle. (1988) *The Politics* (Cambridge, Cambridge University Press).

Australian Bureau of Statistics. (n.d.) https://www.abs.gov.au/articles/religious-affiliation-australia

Australian Government and Australian Institute of Family Studies (AIFS). (March 2022) *Marriages in Australia: Family, Trends and Transitions.* Researchers: Lixia Qu, Jennifer Baxter and Megan Carroll: https://aifs.gov.au/facts-and-figures/marriages-australia

Barnes, Albert. (1834) *Barnes' Notes on the Bible.* [Barnes 1798–1870]. Available at Bible Hub, Online Bible Study Suite: https://biblehub.com/

Barnett, Paul. (2011) *Focus on the Bible, 1 Corinthians – Holiness and Hope of a Rescued People* (Christian Focus Publications). Available at Bible Hub, Online Bible Study Suite: https://biblehub.com/

Barth, Karl. (1958) *Church Dogmatics* (Edinburgh, T. and T. Clark).

Benson, Rev Joseph. (1857) *Commentary on the Old and New Testaments* (2nd edn. 1811-1818. Republished in New York, T. Carlton and J. Porter). [Benson 1749–1821]. Available at Bible Hub, Online Bible Study Suite: https://biblehub.com/

Bible Hub. (n.d.) *Online Bible Study Suite:* https://biblehub.com/

Billy Graham Evangelistic Association. (1 June 2004) "Which of the hundreds of Old Testament laws are applicable to us as Christians?" https://billygraham.org/answer/which-of-the-hundreds-of-old-testament-laws-are-applicable-to-us-as-christians/

Bunyan, John. (1678) *The Pilgrim's Progress* (reprint 1992, Belfast, Ambassador).

Callaway, Kutter. (2018) *Breaking the Marriage Idol: Reconstructing Our Cultural and Spiritual Norms* (Downers Grove, IL, Intervarsity Press).

Canberra Declaration. (n.d.) *Freedom–Family–Faith–Life:* https://canberradeclaration.org.au/

Canberra Declaration. (2010) *Key Signatories:* https://canberradeclaration.org.au/join-us/read-declaration/contributors/

Canberra Declaration. (2018) *The Canberra Declaration:* https://canberradeclaration.org.au/join-us/read-declaration/

Canberra Declaration. (2022) *Campaigns – Standing for Family:* https://canberradeclaration.org.au/campaigns/standing-for-family/

Compelling Truth (2022) "What is the meaning of *phileo* love?" https://www.compellingtruth.org/phileo-love.html

Danylak, Barry. (2010) *Redeeming Singleness – How the Storyline of Scripture Affirms the Single Life* (Wheaton, IL, Crossway).

DePaulo, Bella. (17 Aug 2008) "Is it better to have loved and lost than never to have loved at all?" *Psychology Today*, Sussex Publishers, LLC: https://www.psychologytoday.com/us/blog/living-single/200808/is-it-better-have-loved-and-lost-never-have-loved-all

Ellicott, Charles John. (n.d.) *Ellicott's Commentary for English Readers* (London, Cassell) [Ellicott 1819–1905]. Available at Bible Hub, Online Bible Study Suite: https://biblehub.com/

Erickson, Millard J. (1994) *Christian Theology* (1st edn.). (Grand Rapids, MI, Baker Books).

Erickson, Millard J. (2013) *Christian Theology* (3rd edn.). (Grand Rapids, MI, Baker Academic).

Families Australia. (2022) *Events – National Families Week:* https://familiesaustralia.org.au/events/national-families-week/

Family Voice Australia. (17 May 2021) *The Natural Family is Under Assault:* https://familyvoice.org.au/news?start=5

Focus on the Family. (12 May 2017) "God and Man as Male and Female: Implications for Gender Identity": https://www.focusonthefamily.com/family-qa/god-and-man-as-male-and-female-implications-for-Gender-identity/

Genius [world's biggest collection of song lyrics and music knowledge]: https://Genius.com/

Gill, John. (1746-1763). *Exposition of the Entire Bible* [Gill 1697–1771]. Available at Bible Hub, Online Bible Study Suite: https://biblehub.com/

Glendon, Mary Ann. (2001) *A World Made New* (New York, NY, Random House).

God's Word First (2010) "Defining love in the Bible". Available at: godsword-first.org/fruitofspirit/biblelove-agape-phileo-eros-storge.html

Gundry, Robert H. (2010) *Commentary on the New Testament: Verse-by-Verse Explanations with a Literal Translation* (Peabody, MA, Hendrickson).

Hauerwas, Stanley. (1986) *A Community of Character: Toward a Constructive Christian Social Ethic* (Notre Dame, IN, University of Notre Dame Press).

Hellerman, Joseph H. (30 March 2016) "Our priorities are off when family is more important than church". *Christianity Today:* https://www.christianitytoday.com/ct/2016/august-web-only/if-our-families-are-more-important-than-our-churches-we-nee.html

Henry, Matthew. (1706). *Concise Commentary on the Whole Bible.* (republished 1963, Chicago, IL, Moody Press). [Henry 1662–1714]. Available at Bible Hub, Online Bible Study Suite: https://biblehub.com/

Hourihan, F. (2023) "Australian Singles – A Church and Community Comparison". (Sydney, National Church Life Survey [NCLS] Research).

Hughes, Selwyn. (Sat 5 Feb 2022). *Every Day with Jesus (EDWJ)* (Farnham, Surrey, Waverley Abbey Resources). Jan/Feb 2022.

J. D. Greear Ministries. (30 March 2016) "Why don't we follow all of the Old Testament laws?" https://jdgreear.com/why-dont-we-follow-all-of-the-old-testament-laws/

Jamieson, Robert, Fausset, A. R. and Brown, David (1882) *A Commentary on the Old and New Testaments* (Toledo, OH, J. B. Names and Co.). Available at Bible Hub, *Online Bible Study Suite:* https://biblehub.com/

Jewish Encyclopedia. (1901). https://www.studylight.org/encyclopedias/eng/tje/h/holiness.html

Köstenberger, Andreas J. and Jones, David W. (2010) *God, Marriage and Family: Rebuilding the Biblical Foundation* (2nd edn.) (Wheaton, IL, Crossway).

Leach, Edmund. (1967) *A Runaway World?* (London, BBC [Reith Lectures]).

Mackay, Hugh. (1997) *Generations: Baby Boomers, Their Parents and Their Children* (Sydney, Macmillan).

Mattes, Jane. (1994) *Single Mothers by Choice – A Guidebook for Single Women Who Are Considering or Have Chosen Motherhood* (Harmony).

Meyer, Heinrich August Wilhelm. (1883). *Commentary on the New Testament – Critical and Exegetical* (New York, NY, Funk & Wagnalls).

Morrissette, Mikki (2008) *Choosing Single Motherhood – The Thinking Woman's Guide* (Houghton Mifflin Harcourt).

National Families Week. (2022) "Celebrating the importance of families for 20 years in 2022": https://nfw.org.au/

National Families Week. (2022) "About the week": https://nfw.org.au/about/

New International Version Study Bible. (1985) (Grand Rapids, MI, Zondervan).

Poole, Matthew. (circa 1685) *Poole's Commentary* [Poole 1624–1679].

Pope John Paul II. (2000) *Message.* Family: Dare to Dream Conference, Melbourne.

Prior, David. (1985) *The Message of* 1 Corinthians (London, Intervarsity Press).

Pulpit Commentary. (circa 1890s). Created under direction of Rev J. S. Exell and H. D. M. Spence-Jone. (New York, NY, Toronto, Funk & Wagnalls).

QuoDB. (n.d.) [find any quote in millions of movie lines]: https://www.quodb.com/

Sacks, Jonathan. (1995) *Faith in the Future* (London, Darton, Longman and Todd).

Sands, Paul. (Jan 2010). "The *Imago Dei* as vocation". *Evangelical Quarterly* 82(1), (Exeter, Devon Paternoster Press), pp28-41.

Smalley, Greg. (29 April 2021) "9 reasons to get married": https://www.families.org.au/article/9-reasons-get-married

Sproul, R. C. (22 Jul 2019) "The most solemn mandate". *Biblical Wisdom for Parents:* https://biblical-parenting.org/articles/the-most-solemn-mandate/ Available at Bible Hub, Online Bible Study Suite: https://biblehub.com/

Bibliography

Tennyson, Alfred Lord. (1850) *In Memoriam A. H. H.* (London, Edward Moxon). [poem].

Todd, Margo. (1987). *Christian Humanism and the Puritan Social Order* (Cambridge, Cambridge University Press).

Wesley, John. (1754-65) *Explanatory Notes of the Whole Bible* [J. Wesley 1703–1791].

Wilson, Philip. B. (2005). *Being Single – Insights for Tomorrow's Church* (London, Darton, Longman and Todd).

Yankelovich, D. (1994) "How changes in the economy are reshaping American values". In H. J. Aaron, T. E. Mann and T. Taylor (eds) *Values and Public Policy* (Washington DC, The Brookings Institute).

Zimmermann, Dr A. (26 October 2018) *Christian Foundations of the Australian Law:* Western Australian Legal Theory Association. https://walta.net.au/2018/10/26/christian-foundations-of-the-australian-law/ p8

Note: The material referred to in the above website references was accessible at the time of writing. However, websites and webpages are subject to change at any time and there is no certainty that they will be accessible at any time in the future.

Index

General

Abraham *see Bible characters*
Adam *see Bible characters*
Andrews, Kevin 19, 20, 21, 44, 46, 49–58, 68, 77, 84, 170
Australia/Australian 19, 20, 22, 23, 43, 45, 49, 69–72, 93, 101, 117, 147, 165–169, 199, 216
    Bureau of Statistics (ABS) 22
    census of population and housing 22
    National Census 22, 43, 165, 199, 216
    Government/National Families Week 71
Barth, Karl 109–110
Bible characters
    Adam (first Adam) 54, 58, 102, 107, 114, 116, 120, 122, 133, 135, 144–149, 155, 158, 159, 180
    Abraham 38, 39, 76, 100, 101, 124–127, 130, 133, 134, 141, 152, 154, 186, 211
    Anna the prophetess 178
    Asaph 198, 200

Caesar 107
David, king of Israel 104, 129–133, 200
Elizabeth 53
eunuchs 152, 153, 180–183
Eve 54, 107, 114, 116, 122, 133, 135, 144, 145, 148, 149, 158, 159, 180
Ezekiel 150
Gabriel 132
Hagar 125, 126, 154, 211
Hannah 53
Isaac 126–128, 186
Isaiah 47, 51, 121, 131, 153, 163, 168, 195
Ishmael 126
Jacob (Israel) 128, 132, 148
Jeremiah 130, 132
Jesus Christ *see alphabetical listing*
John the Baptist 53, 178
Joel 140
John 80
Jonah 211
Lydia 178
Mary (mother of Jesus) 132, 133, 143

Mary, Martha and Lazarus 178
Moses 128, 129
Noah 124, 148
Paul 23, 39, 48, 68, 75, 86, 87, 95, 106, 119, 126, 133–135, 140, 148, 154, 160–163, 168, 172, 178–187, 204, 205, 212–215
Peter 83, 131, 140–142, 164, 211, 212
Pharisees 54, 92, 180
Philip the evangelist 178
Rachel 53
Sarah 125, 126, 211
Solomon 130
Satan/serpent/Lucifer/Devil/Prince of this world 64, 123, 124, 133, 159, 160, 172, 175
Timothy 23
British Isles 18, 25, 27, 30–32, 35, 37, 41, 44, 45, 69, 101
celibacy 26–28, 30, 77
Celts 26, 35
church
   American (US) 37
   Australian 43
   British/ British Isles 25, 31, 32, 37
   Christian 35, 40, 42, 101, 170, 178, 199
   Medieval 28
   Presbyterian (Ireland) 25
   Protestant 30–33, 38
   Reformed 29
   Roman Catholic 29, 30, 32, 37
   sanctuary 201–203
   Western 19, 41, 77, 167, 175

Christian/Christianity 20, 23, 26–28, 35, 39, 54, 113, 165, 167, 169, 200, 202, 208, 212
Creation 54, 62, 75, 78–83, 92, 104–116, 122, 123, 144, 148, 158, 181, 193
   Garden of Eden/the 'Fall' 105, 107, 122–124, 133, 158, 159
   man's dominion 111, 112, 123
   the beginning 54, 92, 104, 123, 124, 130, 132, 134, 139–154, 158, 164, 166, 192, 196
Danylak, Barry 184, 185
Darwin, Charles 35
David, king of Israel *see Bible characters*
DePaulo, Bella 190
Egypt 125, 128, 129
Erickson, Millard.J 18, 64, 105–113, 116
Eudaimonia 33, 57, 83
Europe/European 29, 32
family/families
   and rise and fall of nations 61, 83–84
   as building blocks of society 74, 95
   as cornerstone/foundation/foundational institution of society 57, 60, 71, 72, 75, 77, 78, 82, 88, 170
   as greatest hope of humanity 57–60, 71, 84, 88, 135, 169–175
   as a target 88, 89, 95, 171–175
   love for 68, 86, 87, 95, 98–101, 169, 186, 215
   nuclear 26, 32, 33, 37, 45, 56
   nuclear industrial 30

Index

Focus on the Family 118–119
Gentiles 134, 194
God/Yahweh
    image of God 104–120
    our Helper (*'ezer*) 144–146
    reconciliation with/ministry of
        50, 62, 63, 84,
        121–123, 136, 140,
        160, 164, 193, 194,
        203
    worshipping God 30, 202, 203
God's:
    command 78, 111, 130,
        148–151, 158, 163
    covenant
        Old Covenant/covenant law
            126, 129, 133, 154,
            161, 162, 212, 214
        New Covenant 132, 134,
            153, 162, 212, 213,
            215
    enemies (of God/the church) 64,
        188, 89, 60, 170–175
    law/moral law 79, 80, 132, 150,
        160, 162–165
    love 16, 67, 68, 79, 80, 86, 87,
        95, 106, 204, 205
    order for marriage 54, 59, 69,
        86, 92, 93, 104, 137,
        190
Hauerwas, Stanley 40, 166, 175
Hellerman, Joseph H. 77
Holy Spirit 120, 202, 216
    born of 85, 102, 140, 142, 214,
        215
    gifts of 150, 178–188
    guidance 48, 49, 102, 165, 198
    indwelling 145–147, 213, 214
    power 140, 145
Hourihan, Fleur 19, 22, 43
Hughes, Selwyn 159

Israel/Israelites 38, 39, 56, 64, 70,
    76, 104, 121–144, 150,
    152, 162, 194, 202, 212,
    214
Jesus
    cross 48, 49, 64, 73, 88, 89,
        160, 175
    last Adam 58, 102, 135
    parables
        vine and branches 198
        wedding banquet 193–197
        wise and foolish builder 65,
            72, 172
    resurrection 39, 139, 140, 145,
        164
    Son of God 62–64, 97, 127–129,
        136, 141, 149, 154, 215
Judeo-Christian heritage 55, 69, 70
Köstenberger, Andreas J. and Jones,
    David W. 19, 44, 46, 55, 68,
    157, 184
'Last days' 63, 134, 139–148, 202
    Pentecost 131, 140, 141
Luther, Martin 29. 30
Mackay, Hugh 49, 50, 165
marriage
    expected/normal in the church
        30, 31, 40, 44, 52, 53,
        101, 102, 149, 150, 178,
        179, 188, 208
    as greatest desire, hope and
        purpose 34, 57–60, 71, 84,
        88, 135, 167–175
    as vocation 31, 34
    marriage and family breakdown
        15, 45, 46, 50, 56, 60,
        69, 73, 78, 86, 96, 170,
        174, 191
    childless 21, 39, 53, 60, 71, 72,
        74, 125, 149–153
    de facto 92, 94

divorce 23, 36, 54, 69, 93, 94, 180, 181, 182, 190–192
   forbidding 87
   same sex 93, 94
   sanctity of 137
   vows 190
Mead, Margaret 96
monastery/monasticism 27–31, 35
National Church Life Survey (NCLS) 19, 22, 23, 43, 45, 101, 177, 203, 216
Noah *see Biblical characters*
philosophies/philosophers
   Aristotle 32,33,57,74,75,83,169
   capitalism 33
   'Christian humanism' 32
   deconstructionist 55–62, 69, 170–175
   Erasmus 32, 169
   favouritism of marriage and families 17–19, 33, 56–61, 71, 86, 173, 174
   Greek 33, 47, 50, 54
   libertarian 55
   of Michel Foucault and Jacques Derrida 55
   of Edmund Leach 56
   of Libby and Whitehurst 56
   postmodernist 36, 55
   spectrum of secular ideas 56–61, 72, 173–175
Pope John Paul II 96, 97
Prior, David 184
Puritans 30–32, 34
   Bunyan, John/Pilgrim's Progress 30, 31, 34
Queen Victoria 34
Reformation 29–32

sacraments 28, 29
   baptism 29
   communion 29
   marriage 28
Sands, Paul 115
sin
   power of 123, 163, 164
   slave of 58, 123, 128, 129, 154
singleness
   'charisma' of 150, 184, 185
   gift of 150, 178–188
society
   decline of 50, 62, 69, 73, 80, 81, 84, 96
   first consumer society 35
   Victorian England 34, 167
   Western 44, 68, 91–93, 157, 167, 169
social research 19–22, 46 -51, 53, 57, 58, 65, 71, 77, 84, 96
soul friendship 28
Tennyson, Alfred Lord 189–192
Todd, Margo 32
Toynbee, Arnold 83
Wesley, John 98
Wilson, Philip B. 18, 20, 25–42, 44, 45, 55, 56, 68, 101, 166, 167, 170, 175, 211, 215
World War II 49
Yankelovich, Daniel 49, 165

www.ingramcontent.com/pod-product-compliance
Lightning Source LLC
Chambersburg PA
CBHW030253010526
44107CB00053B/1697